DON'T MISS THE MIRACLES

Roy E. Schameck

April M. Schameck

Heather Goodyear

To Aaron, Prayer Partner
Roy was blessed seeing how the
Lord is guiding your ministry.
You, Amanda, Noah, Hannah,
Saphia, and your mom are
precious to us. Thank you
for endorsing our book.
In Christ,
April

DON'T MISS THE MIRACLES

By Heather Goodyear
and
Roy & April Schrameck

CROSSLINK
PUBLISHING

Don't Miss the Miracles

℘ CrossLink Publishing
  www.crosslinkpublishing.com

Copyright, © 2016 Heather Goodyear and Roy & April Schrameck

ISBN 978-1-63357-093-1

Library of Congress Control Number: 2016956989

DEDICATION

To the glory of God for His grace and blessings,
To the caring team of doctors He has put in our path who
know that they treat but He heals,
To our faithful Prayer Warriors, and
To our precious family.

Thanks,
Mom and Dad

CONTENTS

PREFACE

"So, are you ready to write a book?"

These were the first words Dad spoke to me when I saw him again after his life-saving surgery. I walked into the hospital room and he looked up in major pain hooked up to monitors, pumps, and devices. Dad half smiled and asked me that question.

People always put a lot of value in the last words someone has a chance to speak; the wisdom tied up in what those would be if you knew they were your last words on Earth. I would say the first words someone speaks when they realize the awesome fact that God chose to continue their life on Earth hold a lot of value, too. The reality of God's hand and His power to sustain physical life over the last three days was beginning to set in and I'm sure Dad was awestruck.

This was not Dad's first critical health situation, not his first time to thank God for the blessing of a life that could continue to glorify Him, not the first answer of "yes" to prayers offered up to heal Dad. This was even bigger.

Because Dad and Mom have had quite a ministry through all his health problems, I think he realized if he was actually going to get better now his ministry field would have to expand. If his days of lying in hospitals, meeting people in waiting rooms, and witnessing to doctors and staff were at an end, then Dad and Mom needed a new mission field because this was a big story to tell.

My guess is that was what brought his question out. After the expected mental jump back in my head of, "Me?" I knew the question was an important one to step up and answer with action.

Does God still do miracles? Do we have a right to call this one? Why Dad, Mom, and our family? Why would we presume He chose to involve us in one? Why not just give credit to the doctors, wise medical decisions, and Dad's fighting spirit?

The word "miracle" seems like a bold statement. It seems presumptuous and prideful to claim. But God is God, He is eternal, and He still acts today as He always has in the past and always will in the future.

Your very life itself is a miracle. If you've trusted Jesus as your Savior, it's another miracle. We hope you can read our story and learn to see God still does miracles every day. As you allow yourself to get past the cynicism, science, and self-pride that all mask us from seeing them, we bet you will see more and more of God's hand in your life and you won't miss the miracles.

INTRODUCTION

Football, war, and God's Word: all things my family likes to analyze and debate. We enjoy good discussions and digging into the reasons and the "whys" of circumstances and events. Countless discussions around Mom and Dad's dining room table have involved these three topics. Now our older children will jump right in on the same.

During our family discussions, we each make a lot of analogies and comparisons to try to explain circumstances and get our message into just the right words so that the others will understand exactly what we mean to say. After all, isn't that what everyone wants—people to really get what one is saying?

Since we've spent so much time comparing life events to football and wars, and lining them up with God's Word, we want to do the same in our telling of the miracle God did for us. If you want a light and interesting story from this book, read only the football analogies. If you want an inspiring, look-what-the-human-spirit-is-capable-of story, you can read just the war stories and analogies. Our prayer is you will want to read and see the examples from God's Word that point every event to glorifying Him.

CHAPTER ONE

Football - Backs against the wall
War - Surrounded by the enemy
God's Word - The hour of desperation

A dig-in, hang-on moment in any football game is a goal-line stand. The defense is backed up, crouched at the line of their own goal, trying with all their physical might and smarts to not let the other team gain an inch. If the offense gets past and scores, they will at least gain an advantage or maybe even win the game. If the defense holds the offense out, it is always a turning point and a huge morale boost.

Early morning, January 27, 2013, had Dad backed against the goal line. His body was pushing back so hard at the methicillin-resistant Staphylococcus aureus (MRSA) pain closing in on him that his mind couldn't function. Ask my dad about January 27, 2013 and he won't remember much before eight o'clock that night. Ask Mom and my brothers, Craig and Jeff, about January 27, 2013 and they'll tell you they watched Dad make a goal-line stand all day long. Their part was agonizing mentally, like the offense watching their defense on the field. Dad's part was agonizing physically. If he didn't dig in, if he let the pain gain one more inch on him, he would lose the game.

This game of Dad vs. MRSA had been going on for a year. It had been a back-and-forth battle and I'd known from the start Dad didn't want to lose. MRSA is like the football franchise you can't stand because they dominate and win, and they're obnoxious about it. No one wants to lose to that kind of opponent.

When Dad woke up sane at eight o'clock that night, we knew he had kept the other team out of the end zone. My older brother, Craig, called me on his way home from the hospital that night and I could tell the stand had been draining but we were on a turning point to somewhere and the morale boost, even if "cautiously optimistic" (a new favorite saying in our family), was there. Dad could rest shortly on the sidelines, thanks to painkillers and medical staff, and get his strength back before heading back out on the field again.

Similar to a goal-line stand, when the opposition is right up against you, there are times in a war where the enemy is surrounding you. The enemy encircles and you are smack in the middle feeling closed in by the pressure. There's a good chance you can't even see the enemy but you know they are getting close.

How do you strike? Where's the way out? Where's the weak spot to attack? What's the best hope for survival? No matter the answers, it's going to take a fight.

A story about George Washington in 1755 during the French and Indian War is sometimes still told in schools and is documented in the intro movie shown at the beginning of a visit to Mt. Vernon. George Washington was riding with English General Edward Braddock and his troops through the Allegheny Mountain wilderness in Pennsylvania along the Monongahela River. He warned the general and others of the danger of Indian tribes hiding in the trees and even suggested the British should not march in strict formation right through the woods.

On that march they were surprise-attacked by Indians in the thick forest, General Braddock and many officers were mortally wounded, and the troops began to scatter. In the chaos, young George Washington rallied as many men as he could and fought off the enemy. Two horses were shot out from under him, and bullets pierced through his coat, but he fought his way out.

Who knew 143 years later our family's favorite amusement park would be built at the battle site? It seems an unbelievable paradox that we now jump on roller coasters where George Washington rallied as many soldiers as he could to get out alive. There's even a statue of General Braddock right by the Kangaroo ride where we scream and fall into each other as we bounce over the big bump.

The point is that in 1755, God did a miracle in many lives, including George Washington's, in the midst of the war against a surprise attack by an enemy who knew exactly where the weak spot was to attack. Dad and the rest of us have learned MRSA is an enemy who knows how to attack the weak spot.

Years of prednisone-resistant asthma have weakened Dad's bones and immune system terribly. Spontaneous fractures due to weak bones have caused Dad pain many times. Once the MRSA got into his body, it ran around his bloodstream for a while looking for the weak spots. Before Dad even knew the enemy was there, it had set up camp. The obvious weak spot was his lungs, compromised by the years of asthma, so the MRSA started its attack with a little pneumonia. When the pneumonia was cultured, we knew the MRSA was there but we had no idea who this enemy really was. The only thing we knew was we needed to keep the MRSA out of Dad's bones. Like Washington knowing they needed to be aware in the woods, we knew a surprise attack on Dad's bones could be deadly.

We rallied the best defense we knew, which was to start with prayer. Let all the qualified doctors do their jobs and keep us medically informed and we could pray. God put Psalm 34 in my path and it became a passage I read and prayed each day. Verses 19 and 20—"A righteous man may have many troubles, but the Lord delivers him from them all; he protects all his bones, not one of them will be broken"—gave us hope and a knowledge that God cares about and watches over the righteous; even Dad's bones we were so worried about protecting. God's plan was to protect those bones for a whole year.

I remember the phone call when Dad told me the latest MRI looked like the MRSA was in his backbone. It was the surprise attack we'd prayed wouldn't come. For five minutes previously, I thought my worst problem was the hand I had just severely burned on a 350-degree cookie sheet. I was hanging over the sink running cool water over my stinging hand, phone at my ear with my other hand as Dad, nonchalant as always, told me the news. I know Mom and Dad couldn't see my head hanging over the sink or hear my quiet bawling as I mumbled okays and uh-huhs because I would never let them see or hear that. But a thought I had in the midst of this was how quickly my burning, blistering hand meant nothing. Dad had been leveled by the enemy, and that hurt me much more.

Once any initial shock wears off and there is time to sit back and gain a little perspective, a Christian can realize that no sneak attack surprises God. Romans 8:38–39 reads, "For I am convinced that neither death nor life, neither angels nor demons, neither the present nor the future, nor any powers, neither height nor depth, nor anything else in all creation, will be able to separate us from the love of God that is in Christ Jesus our Lord."

Finding yourself facing any of these as an opponent could put a person at an hour of desperation. And that hour could drag on to become days, months, and a lifestyle if we don't focus on the last part of those verses, which is that in any hour of desperation, we are not separate from the love of God. He is not surprised to find us in that circumstance, He is not unprepared for it, and we can be confident that in His love He will either pull us through it or pull us to heaven. Either way we win.

CHAPTER TWO

Football - Set the line up
War - Rally the troops
God's Word - God-given gifts

Our family is part of the fantasy football craze. I must say a few of us are even a little too crazed about the craze. It sparks a certain competitive gene that I see cropping up in my oldest daughter, Emily, and my oldest son, Joseph, who now manage teams in our family league. Truth be told, if it wasn't a family thing I'd be out in a second because, after each Draft Day, the allure is pretty much done for me. I think there's a connection between that and my team's usual two and twelve record up until last year when Emily took over the bulk of the draft research.

But Draft Day is fun. We all scrutinize draft magazines and websites for a week before—taking notes, highlighting player schedules and characteristics, and ranking who we want to try and get on our team at what position and in which round. One late summer afternoon we all crowd around Mom and Dad's dining room table, which then becomes a sheer mess of papers, pens, sticky notes, magazines, and laptops. We pick numbers to see who gets first pick and for the next two to three hours, as each person takes their turns of two-minute picks, we assemble what we each hope will be a successful team for the next season.

On Draft Day in the summer of 2012, MRSA was already racking Dad's body and it was very painful for him to sit up for minutes, not to mention hours. He likes fantasy football that much. We joked about many of the picks he made for his and Mom's teams under the influence of painkillers, because all the picking on each other is also part of the family fun.

Fantasy football is played, I would guess, by millions of people. Each analyst differs a little in the best draft strategy (none of which include being on painkillers), but the general idea is that you want the best player possible at each position based on that player's statistics. You want the running back who runs for the most yards and doesn't share a lot of carries with another teammate. You want the tight end with good strong hands who the quarterback is always looking for in a pinch. You want the quarterback who throws for and completes the long yardage passes. Even better if those passes get completed in the end zone.

That strategy is most likely very successful from a pure game of football point of view for everyone else. The best player stats equal the best line up to choose from each week. However, Emily and I take a different line on Draft Day. As we plan our strategy the week before Draft Day, we look deeper than the stats.

We want the soon-to-be stars who haven't been tainted by the money and success of the game yet. We want the hard workers who just do their job on the field and don't showboat about it. If a player's been suspected or convicted of a DUI, drug charge, domestic violence, or done jail time, there's no place for them in our lineup. Our family knows there's a couple teams we refuse to draft from just because we consider their entire franchise attitude to be thugs or whiners.

Does this make it a little easier on other teams in our league? Probably. Does it make them chuckle that we have a moral standard for our fantasy players? Yes. But when it comes to setting our team lineup each week before the real life games are played out, we feel good about the players we put in. We want to see them use their athletic abilities to play well and rise to the occasion even if on paper they don't appear to be elite at their positions. The added bonus in the end is most of the other family teams in our league also get excited when we do good and never begrudge us the wins we do come up with. They never feel as upset or competitive about losing to us as they do the fantasy powerhouse teams that rack up boring win after win.

Football is always likened to a battle. Not that any of us think a football player's job ever comes close to the job a soldier is doing in battle. One is a game, one is war. I think the analogies come about because of the similar mental and physical requirements to prepare and then dig in and fight. In football, a coach sets a lineup to choose who will head out on the field together. In a battle, the troops are rallied by their commander and assembled to fight alongside each other.

America has fought many important wars, and all of them began with a rallying of the troops. A call for those who would band together and face the enemy. Not every man who faced that call historically was physically superior or an expert marksman. We may read about some of those throughout history who, when it came time to fight, were innately excellent at their position. The soldier stories that really inspire others, though, are those who, when it came time to rally the troops, answered the call out of loyalty and a sense of moral duty.

Michael Uhrich was born in 1751 in Dauphin County, Pennsylvania, and when the time came to defend the colonies for independence, he did his part as a private fourth class in the Fourth Company of the 2nd Battalion of the Lancaster County

Militia. We know Michael Uhrich signed up early to fight because the documentation we have of his service is from a Moravian Congregation church record dated August 8, 1776, and it states:

> *"Yesterday two companies of troops from the Seratora, and today the last company from the town marched for the Army. Numbers of our members called to take leave; Adam Orth and son, John, Michael Uhrich, George Volk, and Henry Boekler. Our evening service was not held in the chapel, owing to so many members being in the army."*

Before enlisting in the army, Michael Uhrich was a farmer and shoemaker. He was married and already the father of one child. Thus far no war accounts tell of any excellent soldier skills that he possessed prior to his enlistment. We do know he survived the Revolutionary War, had a total of eight children, and moved to Ohio where he built the very first mill in the area and began a settlement that became Uhrichsville, Ohio. In the *Historical Atlas, Tuscarawas County, Ohio 1875 and 1908 Combined* accounts of the 1800s, it says about Michael Uhrich,

> *"[He was] an energetic, useful man who lived up to the full measure of his opportunities in moral and civic duties until his death on August 14, 1817."*

We don't know if he was an excellent marksman or physically superior in battle. More importantly, though, what we do have documented through history about Michael Uhrich is that in the rallying of the troops for independence, and then throughout the rest of his life, he had a moral conviction to serve in whatever capacity he could—the type of man who would be valued by officers ranking above him because they knew in a battle his sense of morality and duty would allow him to be one to be counted on.

We also know that Michael Uhrich is my husband's great, great, great, great, great grandfather on his dad's side. That makes his soldier story very inspiring to my children and me. God's plan is not for every person to be called into an actual physical battle of war but we will all be called into many other kinds of battles in this life and how we answer those rally calls will determine the moral legacy that we leave behind.

On January 27, 2013, Dad needed a major rallying of the troops. It had been done before in crises and, as in any crisis, we knew who to call—family. Mom and Dad have both mentioned many times that as a unit, my brothers and I are a force to be reckoned with. Get us focused on a need, especially one of Mom's and Dad's, and it might not be a good idea to stand in our way. We know God has given each of us our strengths and, when needed, that's what we coordinate.

Craig is an amazing police officer and EMT. No one can do what he does, how he does it, and in any medical crisis you want him there. Jeff, my younger brother, is a prosecutor who you don't want to defend against. If Mom or Dad needs something, he'll hunt it or you down. He'll make sure no piece of anything they need at that moment is missing. My part seems to be coordination. Asking the questions to make sure details are covered and keeping everyone informed.

It was actually Mom who sent out the call early that Sunday morning. Craig and Jeff, whose skills were needed immediately so thankfully live closer, arrived first. Mom had called early, before my family and I went to church, to tell me Dad was not doing well and that this was a different kind of not doing well. They were already at the emergency room in Michigan but she had no answers. I left for church with God placing in my mind that those answers, when they did come, were going to shake us.

After the first service, I went out to the car with our youngest daughter, Hannah, and called Mom. The answer I received was of her in the back of the ambulance with my dad in transport to another hospital, and nothing in the background sounded good. I asked her if we should come right away and Mom, who never wants to inconvenience us, tried to mention every reason why it would be hard to make the trip. I, knowing Dad is always thinking first about Mom, asked if Dad wanted us to come. I'm not sure how, other than God, but when she asked him, he was coherent enough to raise his hand in a "yes" response.

My husband, Chris, is not at all in the habit of texting in church but, within a minute of me hanging up the phone, I got a message from him asking if I had heard from Mom. I answered, "Yes, and the kids and I are leaving as soon as the service is done." A minute later he and our other children, them in shock from having walked out in the middle of church, were out the door to meet me.

We lived twenty minutes from our church but within the hour we were home, six of us packed, and already on the road to Michigan. That's the kids' record and they're proud of it! I had told them to pack for a week. We didn't know this rally call wouldn't see us home for another six.

The phrase "rally the troops" means to assemble your allies and get everyone focused on the common goal. When each person has the right end vision, then each person can use their God-given abilities to best reach that goal. Romans 12:4–8 reads, "Just as each of us has one body with many members, and these members do not all have the same function, so in Christ we who are many form one body, and each member belongs to all the others. We have different gifts, according to the grace given us. If a man's gift is prophesying, let him use it in proportion to his faith. If it is serving, let him serve; if it is teaching, let him teach; if it is encouraging, let him encourage; if it is contributing to the needs of others, let him give generously; if it is leadership, let him govern diligently; if it is showing mercy, let him do it cheerfully."

Even before Christ's death on the cross, when the Holy Spirit could indwell believers, the Old Testament tells of events when God would lay His Spirit on individuals for a time in order to equip them to accomplish a task. The building of the Tabernacle by the Israelites in the wilderness was a monumental undertaking. The book of Exodus in chapter 31:1–5 records how God laid His Spirit on Bezalel son of Uri to have the skill and knowledge to build what would be God's dwelling among the people in the wilderness. Not only Bezalel, but God also equipped others with special knowledge that enabled them to work together to reach their common goal.

Jesus promised that after his death and resurrection when he returned to heaven, God would send the Holy Spirit. John 14:26 reads, "But the Advocate, the Holy Spirit whom the Father will send in my name, will teach you all things and will remind you of everything I have said to you." When the crowd Peter spoke to after Jesus had returned to heaven realized they really had crucified the son of God, they wondered what they should do. Peter told them, "Repent and be baptized, every one of you, in the name of Jesus Christ for the forgiveness of your sins. And you will receive the gift of the Holy Spirit. The promise is for you and your children and for all who are far off- for all whom the Lord our God will call." (Acts 2:38–39)

God was not deserting mankind to make it on their own by calling Jesus back to heaven, He was rallying help from heaven to assist each believer. The very Spirit of God. The God who created the world, sent and receded a worldwide flood, and raised the dead to life. That is the same power that as a believer we have in each of us. We should never underestimate that. Unfortunately, more often than not, we do.

CHAPTER THREE

Football - You don't win by thinking you'll lose
War - Stand in the line of fire
God's Word - When God says, "Go."

You have to go into a game thinking you will win. More than thinking you are going to win, you have to back up the attitude with action, and more than that, hard work. While watching a football game, it is easy to tell if one team didn't really show up to play. If a team decides mediocrity is all that's needed that day, it's soon evident.

How many championships have seen the underdog come out on top because they believed they could win and then they played like a team that could? Meanwhile the higher-ranked team had the right "we will win" thought but didn't put any work behind it. They figured they could walk on the field, throw a few easy completions, run a couple easy runs, and be done. The problem is by the time they get over the surprise the underdog is dealing them, it is often too late to recover.

Many football players, especially those considered to be stars, have a bad habit of running off at the mouth. "Verbal diarrhea,"

Dad calls it. They make big boasts before a game and promise great achievements in the week to come, most often at what they swear will be the demoralizing expense of whichever team they are scheduled to play.

There's nothing wrong with a confident attitude of "I can win," "I can make big plays," but it becomes wrong when that attitude loses any sort of the humbleness that should accompany it. Once the humbleness is gone, the player no longer thinks there needs to be any work involved on his part to achieve the win. The humble attitude has been replaced by a sense of entitlement that no longer says, "I can win" but "I deserve to win." When the player feels entitled to win, all sense of personal responsibility in earning that win is gone. When he doesn't win it's not because he did or didn't do anything on the field, it's because *someone else didn't do their job.*

The offense can blame the defense, and vice versa. The quarterback can blame the offensive line or the receivers. The running back can blame the same. The player with all the boasts just days ago now runs off at the mouth in press conferences, on social media, or sports radio, letting the public know it is not he to blame that his team didn't get the win he was entitled to.

It would be nice if this illustration only applied to football, but unfortunately, it seems to be the general attitude of a big part of our population today. In the business world, education world, or in raising children, people want all the winning benefits without ever having to put any work into it. They feel entitled to big bonuses and perks, a diploma or degree, respectful and motivated children, but never want to put in the work involved that must come first to achieve these. Then, like the football player, they complain about all the circumstances and reasons why they don't have what is owed to them. There was a time when the general attitude of America was not entitlement. Instead there was an attitude of if you want to achieve something, first believe you can, and then go work until you do.

There's a difference in wars fought wherein one side believes the way of life they are willing to stand in the line of fire for is right and just for all people as compared to a war fought when one side is rebelling because they don't feel like they are receiving what is owed them. The people of the North in the Civil War believed there were many things about their way of life that made it more right and just for all people than the way of life in the South, and they wanted a united country that stood for those principles.

In 1861 President Lincoln sent out a call for 300,000 troops willing to defend the Union. Because of the way wars were fought at the time, these men would literally be standing in the line of fire to defend their country. Most battles began with men lined up shoulder to shoulder to face gun and cannon fire from the opposite side. In answer to President Lincoln's call, men from around the area of Easton, Pennsylvania, assembled a response of volunteers larger than in any other area of the country. One of the regiments assembled was the 153rd Pennsylvania whose members all came from Northampton County.

The 153rd Pennsylvania mustered in during September of 1862 at Easton for nine months of service and left to defend Washington, DC. They marched many miles and fought valiantly at Chancellorsville where they stood firm on the extreme flank of the Union forces and were able to, in their first artillery battle, fire at least one volley before being forced back by Southern fire from Stonewall Jackson's troops.

Many more miles of marching eventually led them back north to be part of the Battle of Gettysburg. By the time of the battle at Gettysburg, the 153rd's enlistment time was technically up. They could've gotten lazy, they could have complained that they should no longer be in service, but they didn't. Instead they again fought bravely defending the Union values; bravely to the point of a very high mortality rate among their regiment.

The inscription on one of the monuments dedicated to the 153rd on the grounds of Gettysburg reads:

July 1. The Regiment held this position in the afternoon until the Corps was outflanked and retired, when it took position along the lane at the foot of East Cemetery Hill, where it remained until the close of the battle, assisting to repulse the enemy's assault on the night of the 2nd.

Carried into action 24 officers 545 men. Killed and died of wounds 10 officers 40 men. Wounded 7 officers 117 men. Captured or missing 46 men. Total loss 211.

Bordering the grounds of Gettysburg is land that, at the time of the Civil War, belonged to a family named Spangler. In a matter of hours before the beginning of the battle, their land was taken over as an artillery depot for the Union Army and then as the hospital for the 11 Corps, which included the 153rd.

Our family has visited the Spangler Barn site and heard the retelling of many of the stories of the hundreds of men, Union and Confederate, wounded in the battle and taken to the Spangler land. The stories specifically from the wounded men of the 153rd that we heard exhibited continued bravery during very personal suffering as they lay on the grounds of the farm, some outside in the rain, not knowing if it would be their time to live or die. Yet, in the accounts retold to us so those of us now could know the horrors, there is only matter-of-fact reporting of the deplorable situation around them. There is no whining or complaining in their accounts.

From their volunteer enlistment, through the many miles marched, through those wounded, captured, and those who survived the battle and continued to pursue General Lee's men for another week after Gettysburg, the men of the 153rd believed victory involved work, believed they could win, and, therefore they were a part of an important and now famous victory for the North.

When the 153rd Pennsylvania arrived back in Easton in late July 1863, their train was met by thousands of people. A grand heroes' welcome greeted them because they were heroes. The celebration involved banners, music, parades, and reunions with family and friends. These men had sacrificed physically and economically, seen horrible suffering among fellow soldiers, and fought in battle for their country. The 153rd's enlistment was done.

What happened to the men who returned home to the heroes' welcome? Did they live entitled lives expecting gratitude and favors for their time at war? We know a little of the story of one man, Richard Warner, who served in Company I of the 153rd Pennsylvania because we had the pleasure of meeting his great granddaughter a few years ago. His family still remains in Northampton County today, and his great granddaughter is a wonderful historian who proudly possesses Richard's discharge papers and the hat and sword that he would wear in parades commemorating his service in the Civil War. When Richard returned from the war, even after having been wounded on the first day of battle at Gettysburg, he returned to his prewar life of hard work and family; not one filled with entitlement or needing his ego fed because he considered himself better than others.

There are times in life where God is going to lead you into a circumstance and say, "Go." "Go fight," "Go work," "Go do this for my glory." When that happens, our attitudes of we-can-win are of utmost importance. Not the cocky I-deserve-to-win attitude but the humble, with God's grace, if He wills, I-can-do-this kind of attitude.

No matter the pain my Dad is in continuously—no matter the disheartening medical reports delivered time after time, no matter that his health status can actually change by the minute—if you ask him, "How are you doing?" his answer will be, "Practically perfect." That's the attitude Dad has daily because he knows God has got him in that circumstance to fight through it, hoping to win and then praise God for the victory.

Numbers chapter 13 through chapter 14, verse 38 contains the story of God telling Moses to send twelve Israelite men to spy out the land of Canaan. This was land that God had already promised to give to the Israelites. The men were just supposed to go see what the land and people were like and bring a report back to the whole Israelite community. God was ready to give them the go-ahead to take over Canaan and begin living in what would be the Israelites' Promised Land.

When the twelve spies returned, their report began with the richness of the land—but they also quickly reported that the people there seemed powerful and the cities fortified. Only two of the twelve spies, Joshua and Caleb, were ready to trust that God was saying, "Go, take the land," and they tried to silence the other spies and convince the Israelite people to have faith. The community as a whole chose instead to let their fear convince them they couldn't answer God's call at that time. Joshua and Caleb were willing to go and they were, eventually, the only two of the Israelites alive at that time to ever enter the Promised Land. The rest who refused to go on faith all died in the wilderness and never received the blessing God wanted for them.

God has blessings He wants to give each one of us, but if we never listen to His urging of "Go," and we never take on faith that we can do the work involved even if it's going to be hard, then we, like the Israelites, will miss out.

Mom's report to us of Dad's condition that Sunday morning and our departure to Michigan led us to a chaotic week full of serious moments, discussions, and decisions. News on Tuesday revealed the MRSA was eating apart Dad's spine in a quick descent. Dad's top-notch infectious disease specialist, who had been battling this MRSA along with them, called Mom in tears because Dad's MRI had changed so quickly and become critical. His lumbar 1 and 2 vertebrae and 1 and 2 discs were completely infiltrated with MRSA. Along with the diagnosis came the news that Dad's choices were a serious surgery his body was in poor condition to survive or, if not surgery, then more frequent days like the Sunday before that would soon kill him.

Dad has a wonderful team of doctors who care very much about him. His respiratory doctor has been praying with him at the end of every appointment for years. His primary physician has told him a few times, especially after Dad survived his lungs being filled with blood clots, that God has a plan for Dad because if not, Dad would be dead by now with all he's been through medically. The specialist who had been helping Dad endure the MRSA pain had driven through a blizzard to the hospital on Sunday to administer the IV medication Dad had needed to calm his body down. Because of these doctors' affection for Dad and Mom, they looked for and searched out all the possible options of surgeons and surgery types. The surgery Dad needed was going to be risky. Any surgeon would need not only ability, but also determination to even attempt the surgery.

On Thursday Dad's doctors' search brought a very young surgeon to Dad's hospital room, and he wasted no time laying out a matter-of-fact plan for Mom and Dad and told them he'd be back Friday for their decision. The surgeon told Dad he was 90 percent sure he could perform the surgery, but only 10 percent sure Dad would stay alive during it. Before leaving, he went to Dad's bedside to shake hands. My dad shook the surgeon's hand and told him, "God bless you." The surgeon held Dad's hand and very seriously looked him in the eyes and answered back, "You, too, Mr. Schrameck." If you're not used to listening to God in every situation, you can miss moments like that.

God knew Dad would really want fellow Christians heading into the operating room with him, and so it was God's grace to reveal to Mom and Dad in His way that this was the guy. This surgeon knew the odds of the battle, knew the length and extent of the work the surgery would take, and still he was willing to be the one to try when others weren't.

Mom and Dad could sense God telling them, "Go." They now had a day to decide to listen on faith and send Dad into surgery, or let fear have them try at all costs to avoid that risk. But, like the Israelites, avoiding the risk could also mean missing the blessings.

CHAPTER FOUR

Football - The Hail Mary
War - Unlikely allies
God's Word - When God's all you've got

Backyard pickup football games are what our family likes to play. Every Thanksgiving growing up involved a morning family football game and sometime during the Christmas week we'd be out in the yard for some snow football. Dad, Craig, Jeff, me, and whatever family was visiting for that holiday had a great time playing in a simple game of two-hand touch.

As we got older, the games got more serious. Simple two-hand touch became semi-tackle with jerseys, cleats, and receiver gloves. Part of our packing for trips back to Mom and Dad's after Chris and I got married included football clothes. I still write "football clothes" on the kids' packing list alongside PJs, outfits, and other necessities when we get ready to visit Nana and Pa's.

When our own kids were old enough to join the games, we coddled them for the first few years with easy hand-offs and wide-open touchdown runs. It was not too long, though, before they learned Uncle Jeff wasn't going to baby them. He soon stopped turning off the afterburners and would blow right past them the same way he'd done to us for years. They learned quickly, too, that a full-contact hit from Uncle Craig hurts badly and he doesn't pull his blocks on account of your age. He sometimes tried to somersault over them when he realized they were a foot away and he was moving at full speed, but even that could result in his foot to their foreheads as he vaulted.

Football plays often have fun names to describe what happens during the play, and one of the trick plays we would try to pull off in our games was the hook and ladder. In the hook and ladder play, a receiver runs downfield, turns back, or hooks for a pass, and then turns and laterals it to the receiver who is sprinting downfield behind him. The play has the appearance of a ladder extending in sections from a big fire truck as each pass is completed in steps along the field.

The most famous play name even a lot of nonfootball fans know is the Hail Mary. The Hail Mary happens at the last moment of the game when the quarterback hurls the ball as high and far as he can to his team's end zone. The idea is that one of the many receivers that sprinted for the end zone will come down with the ball, score a touchdown, and win the game in the final seconds. The play is called the Hail Mary because the ball is literally thrown into the air with a burst of your biggest effort and a prayer that it results in the last-second touchdown you need.

The Hail Mary is a combination of surrender, faith, and hope as the quarterback backpedals, cocks his arm, and lets the ball go. He has no more control over the ball or the game. He gave that up in a last-ditch effort to velocity, trajectory, and whoever awaits the ball on the other end.

A Hail Mary on the field is emotion-filled and exciting for the players, announcer, fans, and even anyone watching who doesn't care at all which team wins. I'd be surprised if even the most casual sports fan doesn't hold their breath while the ball is floating in the air until it is either caught or drops to the field. All excitement aside, and in the scope of what's truly important in life, the outcome of that pass in the end zone does not rank very high. There are other Hail Mary times in life where the outcome matters much more.

Every war movie I can think of has some Hail Mary moment to which the story is building. I know this because growing up, I ended up watching quite a few. Television was not the endless option of channels that it is now. I remember when some networks used to turn off at 10:00 p.m. and the channel turned to static until the next morning when their programming began again. There were only a few stations in existence, and if you wanted to watch a show or movie, you sat down and hunkered in for the duration because there were no VCRs or DVRs. At commercial times you could sprint to the bathroom if you really needed to, but no one was pausing the show for you until you got back.

The other difference about television viewing from when I was young was that each household used to have one TV. Just one. There were none in bedrooms and no computers and handheld devices with streaming capabilities. Just one TV that the whole family watched together. Since everyone was watching together, the old "majority rules" rule was definitely in effect. Mom didn't care much for TV and I was only intrigued by it, so that meant the easy majority fell to Dad and my brothers—and that meant a lot of war movies. Once every few years a network would show *The Sound of Music* or *Mary Poppins* and we'd settle down on the basement floor with bowls of Dad's super buttered popcorn to watch. Other than those, my only memories of movies we hunkered down for are *The Guns of Navarone*, *The Big Red One*, *Bridge Over the River Kwai*, and *The Battle of the Bulge*.

I know I watched *The Battle of the Bulge* at least four times growing up, but until two years ago I had no idea what the battle was actually about in the scope of World War II. The movie, like many of the others, had Germans, tanks, and spies, along with the occasional explosion. That's all my blurry memory knew of its historical significance. I didn't realize, until I studied World War II a bit more, the vast spy networks of brave people involved on both the Axis and Allied sides who risked death to form alliances to either help or hinder the side they were fighting for.

During my kids' and my study of World War II, I mentioned to some friends that while I grew up watching all these war movies, I had no clue what they were actually about other than war in general. I told them I especially hadn't known anything about the Battle of the Bulge except that the name was catchy and so it stuck in my head, but now I actually did know the real significance and I felt so much more educated. That evening I got to feel even more educated when our friend responded by telling us his grandpa, Ray, had fought in the Battle of the Bulge, serving in the 28th Pennsylvania.

More than just an intriguing movie, the Battle of the Bulge, beginning December 16, 1944, was the Germans' last-ditch effort, their Hail Mary attempt, to attack the western front and push the Allies back into Belgium. The Germans picked an unexpected, low-manned spot in the wilderness to attack the American line and went full force at them early on a foggy morning. The battle got its name because as the Germans pushed through the weak spot, they created a big bulge in the Allied forces' line. The attacked center of the line began to cave in toward the west while the unattacked northern and southern lines remained stationary, so an aerial photo would've resembled a big bulge.

With the unexpected full force the Germans unleashed on the outnumbered Allies, plus the English-speaking German soldiers who put on the captured uniforms and infiltrated into the Allied ranks, there was mistrust, chaos, and a large loss of American lives. Ray was not one who lost his life in the battle; he was captured and taken to a Nazi prison camp.

The Battle of the Bulge continued to be fought for three weeks before the Allies began to stabilize the area in their favor again. Since the battle had been the Germans' Hail Mary attempt, and it looked like the ball was going to drop untouched into the end zone, Hitler became especially desperate and there are many reports of the ill treatment of prisoners captured on that western front. Ray would have been mentioned in postwar years in those reports if it weren't for an unlikely ally who threw him and a fellow group of prisoners a Hail Mary.

The first night at the prison camp, a German soldier approached Ray standing among a group of soldiers to inform them that prisoners were going to be executed the next morning at 10:00. The German soldier said, "I go on duty at 9:00. The gate over there will be unlocked (pointing to his left) and I will be looking over there (pointing to his right)." That's all he said.

Imagine the night spent by Ray and fellow prisoners. They were being thrown a Hail Mary. Did they go for it and sneak out the gate? Was this soldier an unlikely ally or a liar? What if the execution squad was actually waiting on the other side of the gate?

The next morning Ray took the word of this unlikely ally. He—and we don't know how many others—walked through the unlocked gate into the wilderness and into a long postwar life. Sometimes in football, war, and life, we've got to throw our hands in the air with a prayer realizing God's all we have. Many a prayer is like the Hail Mary pass when we hurl our situation at God and hope He'll catch it for us.

After the young surgeon's visit on Thursday, January 31, 2013, Mom and Dad had quite an afternoon and night. Mom and Dad, as Mom says a lot, "bathe everything in prayer." This situation was no different. We'd all been praying since the first mention of MRSA a year ago and had definitely increased our prayers over the past five days. This increase in prayer was not because we thought God wasn't hearing us, but because He was truly all we had who was remaining the same.

We learned a wonderful lesson that when information and circumstances around you change within minutes and God is the only constant you know, you are truly blessed. When no aspect of your temporary life is steadfast at the moment and God is the only one you can count on to catch your Hail Mary, He will be in the end zone. The times in life when you can truly hang on the tightest are when the only thing you are hanging on to is God.

I have never directly asked Dad this question, but if I asked him what he lives for, I would say by his actions his answer would be: one, service to God; two, to take care of Mom; and three, to be as big a part as he can of his kids' and grandkids' lives. Even though Dad is a godly man who doesn't cling to this life, if God was giving him an option to continue to do some service on this earth and stay with all of us, then he was going to take it. So Friday brought the decision for surgery.

There are many Bible verses quoted so often in times of crises they now sound cliché. This happens because we pick out only the part of a verse or passage we want to cling to as a promise. Philippians chapter four, verse six, begins by stating, "Do not be anxious about anything." A wonderful sentiment and an ideal for which to strive. It's easy to tell someone, "Well, God says don't be anxious about anything." But with many of God's promises—and because He did not create us as robots but rather He wants a relationship with us—those promises require some action on our part.

We don't need to be anxious about anything when we add on the rest of Philippians 4:6 along with verse seven. "Do not be anxious about anything, but in everything, by prayer and petition, with thanksgiving, present your requests to God. And the peace of God which transcends all understanding will guard your hearts and minds in Christ Jesus."

Mom and Dad have for many years followed this model of prayer, so it was a natural response for them in this situation. When you can wholeheartedly present your requests to God, you will have a peace that enables you to take action and do what needs to be done. It keeps anxiousness from paralyzing you. Anxiousness will render you ineffective to accomplish any decision or task.

Mom and Dad prayed, and continued to pray, as they met with the surgeon, anesthesiologists, and respiratory doctors. They prayed as Dad went through many pre-op tests to target the best area of his spine for attack, and to determine if his heart was strong enough to keep beating during a surgery of this length. We all continued to pray as we had difficult conversations about what would need to be done if Dad didn't wake up after surgery.

One of the mundane but necessary tasks to be done was the witnessing and signing of Dad's will and advanced life directives. If needed he put all decisions into Mom's hands, of course, but that fact needed to be legally documented before the surgery. Many details like the will consumed our few days and nights presurgery, and during that time we still had our kids who needed cared for, fed, and home at Nana and Pa's at some point of the night to sleep in their beds. Our children were watching us closely during these days, and it was important for us to remember that. Because we had the calmness of the Lord, and because Dad is such a calm trooper, they really didn't pick up on the reality of what all was happening.

The need to get the will signed was actually what finally made Emily and Joseph fully realize the seriousness of Dad's condition. Getting papers, a notary, and witnesses together takes coordination anytime, but we had only a day to get them all together at the hospital and it didn't happen until the night before Dad's surgery. God had put Mom and Dad's church secretary, who is a notary, right in the area of the hospital when they called her.

Late into the evening my sister-in-law, Jen, met me in the hospital parking lot with her and Jeff's kids, Julia, Ryan, and Lauren. Their kids hopped in our twelve-passenger van with our kids, and we all drove circles in the dark parking lot for an hour so Jen could run up to Dad's room and be a witness for the will signing.

We spent the hour singing to and critiquing praise songs on the radio to cover up Hannah's screaming from her car seat and Lauren's continual asking for Jen. We were even stopped once in our big green van and asked if we were a transport service. All the noise and driving kept the younger ones oblivious, but Emily and Joseph caught on to the fact that if we were driving circles in the dark, the night before surgery so a bunch of adults could huddle up in Pa's room, then things must be serious.

As humans we will never cease having feelings, and there may always be an underlying anxiousness or worry we are trying to ignore. But once we've given our petitions to God, the peace He promises is there, and it really is amazing. The Bible says, "The peace of God ... transcends all understanding," and it truly does.

To be in a crisis of the unknown and yet have the peace to know you can and will do what needs to be done is an unexplainable feeling because we really don't understand how we have such peace. We have this peace because God promised when we give Him our prayers, our hearts and minds will be guarded in Christ Jesus. The two places where our thoughts and emotions can take over and spiral us into anxiousness are guarded by Christ, replaced with thoughts and emotions of peace.

Dad and Mom were a testimony to this peace through every part of the long week that had begun the previous Sunday. From the decision for surgery to the moment of surgery they exhibited rock solidness. Even Mom who can go down the path of anxiousness showed an amazing matter-of-fact, we're-gonna'-get-this-done attitude during the 48 hours between the decision for surgery and the time to begin it. Dad made time for any hospital worker, relative, or friend who visited his hospital room or talked to him on the phone during those two days, and every one of them heard the credit for Dad's attitude given to prayer and God.

Even though hospitals are notorious for their noise and interruptions just when you want to rest, Dad still had moments in those two days presurgery when he was alone in his hospital room with God. I know Dad spent a lot of those moments petitioning God with a very large anxiety: being on a ventilator. Not much medically puts fear and anxiousness into Dad, but the thought of waking up on a ventilator after surgery always has. It's something he's never wanted, and with all his respiratory issues it's something he worries about. Yet, God's peace was big enough to guard against even that worry. The day before surgery Dad told me, smiling, that he and God had made a deal. The deal was he was not going to wake up on a ventilator. Dad had confidence in that and a peace that would help him relax going into surgery.

The peace of God does not make you immune to feeling emotion. Mom came home for a little the night before the surgery so Dad and she could both get some rest heading into the next day. While Mom and I drove to the hospital the next morning, she told me they had spent a long time on the phone during the night. "We talked, cried a little, and prayed together," she said.

Mom didn't know if she would be a widow that day. Dad couldn't guarantee he would be there to continue their life together. They were both feeling strong emotions heading into surgery, but the peace of God in Christ Jesus was enough to calm even anxieties as big as those.

CHAPTER FIVE

Football - As the clock ticks down
War - In the trenches
God's Word - God is eternal

What actually decides which team wins and which team loses? It's who's ahead when the clock hits 00:00. Important preparations and game execution go into the whole sixty minutes of a football game. Regardless, the team with more points at 00:00 is the winner. As a spectator there is watching and waiting as the game plays out, often a sense of urgency as the fourth quarter counts down, and then a sense of finality at 00:00. Happy or sad, depending on which team you were cheering for, when the clock runs out the game is over.

There's an almost predictable pattern in our family as we watch a game of our favorite team. Even in games that have some implication for standings or playoffs, we are calm at the beginning and sit down on our couches with plates of snacks. We watch pretty calmly through the first and second quarters, discussing plays and getting up for more snacks. The mood in the family room becomes more intense as the third quarter plays out, and then even more as the fourth quarter starts. Into the fourth quarter there is less talk amongst us and less leaving the television to grab snacks. By the last half of the fourth quarter, we are all intent on the TV, standing up and groaning or cheering at every play. We're watching the clock, watching the plays, rocking back and forth, hoping our team is ahead at 00:00.

In really tense games some of us pace, some of us jump. Mom, Joseph, Jeff, and Ryan are all TV yellers. Chris and Emily are play-by-play analyzers believing, it seems, that their comments will make it to the coaches and players. Dad gets annoyed at botched-up crucial plays and questions out loud to all of us why that idiot is on the team. Sometimes I wonder why I watch our favorite team at all because it's three hours of escalating nervous energy and stress. Aren't there enough situations in life that inflict that on me? Why do I purposefully do it to myself every Sunday of football season?

Sunday is an unusual day for surgery, but Dad's surgery was scheduled for Sunday, February 3, 2013. The surgeon knew there would be many rooms available and he wouldn't be rushed through the amount of time the surgery would require. The intriguing thing about Sunday, February 3, 2013, considering my family's enjoyment of football, was that it was Super Bowl Sunday. Super Bowl Sunday and we didn't care.

Had Chris, the kids, and I been in Pennsylvania we would've had a houseful of fifty people. Any other year Mom and Dad would've cooked ham and potato salad and been content to settle in and enjoy the game. Craig and Jeff would've each been with their wives and kids watching the game. The Super Bowl of 2013 just didn't matter to us.

Pregame activities droned on all day from the TV hanging in the corner of the waiting room and we, maybe, commented on them once or twice. We were still waiting out Dad's surgery hours later, well past halftime of the actual game, but none of us could've described what happened at any point of football's biggest game of the year.

The game of football is a common topic of conversation amongst us. My nephews Daniel and Nicholas, Craig's sons, and Ryan all play. Various ones of us watch every level from peewee to pro, and we comment on nuances of games all the time. But even the Super Bowl, one that involved a team most of us vehemently dislike, elicited hardly a glance from us all day. The reason being no matter how crazy any one of us gets about football games from peewee to professional, football is just a game. The only comparison I felt that day to the game we enjoy so much was that when Dad's surgery clock hit 00:00, I wanted him to be ahead.

Football commentators often use the phrase "in the trenches" during the game. The phrase dates back to a type of warfare most well known as the predominant battle strategy in World War I. Many phrases are commonly applied to both football and war, but "in the trenches" when referencing football only gives a glimpse of what full trench warfare really entailed on the battlefield.

A trench in warfare refers to a long narrow hole dug into the ground. During a football game, the players in the trenches are the members of the offensive or defensive line. These players dig their feet in and use their strength to hold their own line. Each player has to bare-handedly overpower an opponent across the line. How the linemen succeed "in the trenches" affects the success of the running and passing plays of a team. The linemen in the trenches do the hard physical work of holding their line to allow for the success of the passers and runners.

The linemen in a football game represent what, in trench warfare, was the first line of three trenches often dug by an army. The first trench, or front line trench, was closest to the opposing army's lines of trenches and the one from where the fighting took place. Soldiers were lined up in the trench waiting for the time they were commanded to fire weapons upon the enemy or rush up over the top to try and overtake the enemy's trench opposite of them through hand-to-hand combat. The front line trench was the most stressful and ready-for-action environment in this type of combat.

The second line of trenches, back from the front line, was the support trench. Soldiers and munitions were in this trench ready to engage in the battle if the front line trench were to be overrun by the enemy. The reserves of men and weapons could be called upon immediately to support the front line men.

Even further back from the front line trench, with the support trench between them, were the troops in the reserves trench. A soldier's rotation usually followed a three-week schedule—one week in the front line trench, one week in the support trench, and one week in the reserve trench. The reserve trench was a place of safety for the soldiers to rest for a time. It did not exclude them from all aspects of war; the trenches were often muddy, narrow, crowded, and lice-filled. Battles being fought up in the front line trenches would not have escaped all notice of those in the reserves, but it was still a place to be sheltered temporarily until a soldier was called again up to the front line.

Because America was not directly involved in World War I until very late in the war, it seems to be the war we are taught least about these days. The heroic stories that most people have heard come out of the American Revolution, Civil War, or World War II. Of course we know there were heroes and sacrifice during World War I, but they've gotten a little lost in our history books.

The heroic moments and sacrifices of World War I often took place in the physically grueling warfare by those in the front line trenches. The letters home and diary accounts were often written during the waiting periods of the soldiers in the reserve trenches. Because of the threefold nature of trench warfare, "in the trenches," when used to describe moments of war, can actually apply two ways. One way means to be directly engaged in a grueling battle.

The other means to be sitting back, protected and waiting. On Dad's day of surgery, we felt both of these applications.

Dad's surgery was scheduled for 11:00 a.m. and Dad wanted us at the hospital at eight o'clock. Each of us in the family has a differing degree of reputation for being late at times, but Sunday morning at eight o'clock we all met in Dad's hospital room, ready to face the battle. Many of us were armed with coffee and some of us were even early—unheard of! It was only Dad who would be in the front line trench that day while the rest of us would be in the reserves, but we converged on Dad's hospital room that morning because he wanted us there. We would support him even in the tiniest way before he headed into battle.

Dad wanted to see us all present and accounted for at the hospital and to ensure we were all there for Mom. We didn't mourn or worry crowded in his hospital room not knowing when a nurse would come wheel his bed down the hall to operating. We just joked around. We made fun of Craig's froo-froo coffee drink, Jeff's constant germaphobia when in any hospital, and talked as if we'd all be together later. Mom and Dad's decision for surgery had been made, the pre-op work had been done, and nothing was going to change the fact that soon Dad would be in the operating room, so we just enjoyed our time together.

Once Dad and his surgeon hit the front line trench, they would face hours of surgery. The surgeon's task was to remove two vertebrae, build two new artificial vertebrae with an antibiotic-treated compound, and then stabilize Dad's spine and spinal cord with metal rods that would run from Dad's mid back into his pelvic bone, cemented and screwed to hold it all together. Dad's one task was to fight to stay alive.

From his hospital room Dad was taken to the pre-op section of the operating wing and once the nurses had him ready, we were all allowed back to talk with him until surgery time when we would head to the reserve trench of the waiting room during Dad's battle. Dad remained calm and matter-of-fact and, as we often do, taking our cues from him, we did, too. We talked about missing the Super Bowl this year, how he'd get a good nap without any pain during the surgery, and what recovery and post-op would entail. Once the surgeon arrived to check in with Dad, and before he left to scrub up, Jeff shook the surgeon's hand and asked, "Are you ready to be part of a miracle today?"

Dad said a prayer with Mom, Craig, Jeff, Chris, and me and then there was no more pre-op time. It was surgery time. We sent Dad into surgery telling him, "Love you," and "We'll see you after," but we all knew the risks. It only takes a second to die, and there are a lot of seconds in a surgery that ended up lasting nine hours. We could have sat in the waiting room counting every second and worrying; instead, God allowed us to do what my brothers, Chris, and I always do when we are together—which is goof around and have fun.

We staked out our own corner of the waiting room and moved chairs and tables around to our liking. We figured we were there for the long haul so we'd get comfortable. Chris, who was put in charge of manning Dad's phone, joked that he was going to send group texts from it throughout the day with surgery updates to freak people out. We discussed if we should change Dad's social media status to "in surgery" or "temporarily unreachable" for the next nine hours.

We have a great picture of my brothers manhandling the vending machine when the almonds Jeff paid for didn't drop down. We cracked up when Craig jumped up and dashed to the vending machine then returned empty-handed and told us he'd seen a Jr. Mint on the floor and was so excited they might have them in the machine, but that someone must've just dropped one the day before to get his hopes up. When we got hungry around dinner, we had a good time with the make-your-own-burrito app Craig found on his phone for a local fast food Mexican place. Our humor and antics were distracting enough even for Mom who said it was a good thing we had half the waiting room to ourselves.

None of this means we weren't jumping every time a door opened or checking the surgery board often to make sure Dad's name was in the color signifying "in surgery." I figured if his name stayed in that color, then he was still holding strong and Jeff, Craig, and I got up to check that board a lot as a small reassurance. Our antics didn't mean we weren't continually offering up silent prayers. Our actions did mean we were relaxed enough to each be sensing God's peace and to have Mom rolling her eyes at all of us.

God gave me the thought that because He isn't bound by our sense of time, He was already in Monday morning. He was either there holding all of us brokenhearted, or He was there helping us help Dad battle back to his feet again. But He wasn't asking us to handle all of that right then, He was just asking us to wait. Countless personal and political wars have been fought throughout time. Whether we know a lot or nothing about each one, God has been present at them all. God is eternal, which means He always has been, He is, and He always will be.

Our earth is full of schedules and events dictated by the units of time humans have set as the standard. I know now that God is bigger than any man-made unit of time. He will sometimes reach down into our concept of time and change everything, or sometimes He will choose to work within it. I have a new respect for the gift and importance of time because God is in the times when everything seems to be falling apart, and He's also in the times when everything seems to come together at just the right moment.

Humans measure time by clocks and calendars, but God measures time by eternity. God identifies the eternal nature of himself in the Old Testament many times when having conversations with people. When speaking to Jacob in the book of Genesis, chapter 28, verse 13, the Bible records, "There above it stood the Lord, and he said: 'I am the Lord, the God of your father Abraham and the God of Isaac. I will give you and your descendants the land on which you are lying.'"

In the book of Exodus, chapter 3, verse 6, God is speaking to Moses about the great miracle He is going to do through the Israelites' exodus. The verse reads, "Then he said, 'I am the God of your father, the God of Abraham, the God of Isaac, and the God of Jacob.' At this, Moses hid his face, because he was afraid to look at God."

After some discussion between God and Moses, God identifies himself again in verses 14 and15, "God said to Moses, 'I AM WHO I AM. This is what you are to say to the Israelites: I AM has sent me to you.'" God also said to Moses, "Say to the Israelites, 'The Lord, the God of your fathers—the God of Abraham, the God of Isaac, and the God of Jacob—has sent me to you. This is my name forever, the name by which I am to be remembered from generation to generation.'"

These events in Genesis and Exodus took place hundreds of years apart but throughout the Old Testament of the Bible God identifies himself in this way to show His eternal faithfulness to His people. He is identifying himself as the God who has been with generations before and usually follows that identification by letting people know what great thing He is going to do. Jacob saw God make his family into an entire nation, the Israelites. Moses saw God perform the events of the Exodus which led the Israelites out of years of slavery in the prominent nation of ancient Egypt.

The Exodus was such a mighty display of God's power that afterward He always referred to it when speaking to the Israelite people as being the "God of the Exodus." This now made God the God of Abraham, Isaac, Jacob, and the God of the Exodus showing His eternal nature to His people. The Israelites eventually referred to God as "I AM." This title was considered very holy and not to be used in addressing any other than God.

When Jesus, the Son of God, who is God, came to earth to die for our sins, He wanted to give the Jewish people (descendants of the Israelites) as much proof as He could that He was the Savior they had read about many times in the Scriptures. When Jesus was speaking to a crowd of Jews in the Jewish temple and telling them about his eternal nature, he said, "I tell you the truth, before Abraham was born, I am!"

The book of John in chapter 8, verse 59 tells us that when Jesus said this, the crowd of Jews picked up stones to stone him. They considered it blasphemous for anyone to refer to himself as "I Am." Jesus was not committing blasphemy, He was trying to show He was the one they'd been waiting on throughout history and that He'd been waiting throughout history to come to earth and die for their sins.

Jesus continued during his ministry to reference himself with the title "I am" using word pictures the Jewish people should have been able to recognize if their hearts and eyes were open to God's teaching. In John chapter 10, verse 11, Jesus said, "I am the good shepherd. The good shepherd lays down his life for the sheep." In John chapter 11, verse 25, Jesus said, "I am the resurrection and the life. He who believes in me will live, even though he dies." Jesus spoke very clearly in John chapter 14, verse 6 when He said, "I am the way and the truth and the life. No one comes to the Father except through me."

God had been waiting since eternity past to send Jesus to reconcile us sinful humans back to Him because He loves us so much. Jesus's death and resurrection were a moment in time when God was bringing everything together to save us from the sin we are born with. God desperately wants, and has always wanted, people past, present, and future to understand and accept Jesus's life and death as the way of forgiveness for our sins so we can spend our eternity with Him. During the long years—and much turmoil—from the Garden of Eden to Jesus's Resurrection, and every moment since, God has been working through time to bring us back from our sins to Him.

During the stressful week of time leading up to Dad's surgery—when it seemed like everything was falling apart—we couldn't see how God was going to bring it all together, but by Sunday morning at 11:00 a.m., He had done just that for us.

11:00 a.m. Sunday. For forty-eight hours that had been "go time" for us. Dad's surgery had been scheduled for 11:00 a.m., but that wasn't actually what God had scheduled for 11:00 a.m.

While Mom, Craig, Jeff, Chris, and I were around Dad back in the pre-op room, we originally thought we would only have a few minutes to talk. We ended up with the gift of all the time we did because at 11:00 a.m., there was no surgeon. About eleven thirty, Dad looked at us and said, "I guess the surgery was scheduled for eleven o'clock to give a lot of people another chance to pray."

God knows what most churches are doing at eleven o'clock on a Sunday morning, and that is starting their service. Mom and Dad's church in Michigan, Jeff's church in Michigan, and our church at the time in Pennsylvania were all starting their services and they all thought to pray for us.

We never heard exactly what words were said in those prayers, but I do know that God hears prayer and responds within His will, and my family knows Sunday went the way it did because people prayed. People in our churches and so many others in Michigan, Pennsylvania, and even Australia prayed to the same God that people have been praying to for all time.

I'm sure some of the prayers were for the surgeon, and God answered those prayers miraculously. Dad's surgery went perfectly, with not a single crisis the entire nine hours. The surgeon was able to do all he had wanted to do in order to give Dad a fighting chance against the disease. After the surgeon came to the waiting room and gave us the report we had been so hoping for, God did yet another amazing thing for us: while we were all smiling, rejoicing, and thanking the surgeon many, many times, Mom and Dad's pastor asked the surgeon if he would like to pray with us. What an experience for all of us to stand in a circle offering thanks to the Lord, and among all of our hands held together were the same hands God had just used to save Dad's life.

I'm sure many of the prayers said that Sunday were for survival. I'm sure part of God's decision to have Dad survive was a direct result of all the prayers. I know we were all at terms with whatever God had planned. Dad knew he was good either way; either he was waking up with the Lord, or he was waking up here to battle back. But I do know it would hurt him very much to leave Mom, because he wants to be here to take care of her and God knows that, too.

God has known since time began He would see Dad and us through the battle of this surgery. He knew He'd be with us in that moment as we joyously gave Him thanks. He also knew He was going to be, and still continues to be, with us through Dad's recovery.

CHAPTER SIX

Football - 20 losses
War - We turn a blind eye
God's Word - Don't be like the Israelites

0 and 20. That was Jeff's varsity football record when he graduated high school. The varsity football team, once a local powerhouse, did not win one game from the middle of Jeff's sophomore year, when he moved up to varsity, through his senior season. That is demoralizing for most high school athletes, and certainly not fun, especially for someone who loves the game as much as he does. There were no Hail Mary moments or victories when the clock ticked down. Only loss after loss, week after week. Week after week of trudging back to the locker room dirty and cold, helmet in hand, with no elation of victory. Even without the glory that comes to a winning high school athlete, even without the Friday night victory celebrations, Jeff still loved the game and played hard every week.

Jeff's interest in football has run deep since he was very young. He began writing self-designed football plays when he was six and compiled notebooks full of them. I'm sure we could dig in some dresser drawer or attic bin at Mom and Dad's and find them. Now on autumn Saturdays he carries a leather folder full of his own plays along the sidelines as he coaches Ryan's teams.

When Jeff was four he suffered second and third degree burns on the lower half of his body. Unfortunately that incident has something to do with him and I jostling each other over some leftover Halloween candy too close to the counter with five large mugs of steaming tea Dad had just poured. Two weeks into his recovery, while he was still fully bandaged from the waist down, Mom was in the basement doing laundry and heard a thumping sound up above. She came upstairs to find Jeff tossing his football up in the air and then hobbling to catch it across the length of our living and dining rooms.

He was bandaged, sore, and burned, but, even at four years old, determined. Instead of lying in bed, he got up to play football. He kept the same attitude Monday through Friday in high school at practice and during the 48 minutes of Friday night games.

The thing about all those losses is that they actually made Jeff a better athlete. He, like Dad, is very strong mentally. He knows, and knew then it seemed, how to take a loss and move on. How to know that, yes, you were defeated in a game, but you don't have to feel defeated as a person.

High school sports can become an athlete's entire identity. When a sport is all that makes you feel good about yourself, suffering a loss means suffering a loss of self. Jeff is supercompetitive. Truthfully he is beyond supercompetitive. Though each loss made him mad, it did not madden him to the point that he couldn't recover and be civil to those around him or get up the next morning and keep trying.

Jeff kept playing football, lost game after lost game, through high school and then one day, three years later, his college football team won the Division III National Championship. Loss after loss, if we hang in long enough, will eventually lead to some big victory.

Dad had suffered medical setback after medical setback during his battle with MRSA. He'd had two painful shoulder surgeries as the MRSA ate his shoulders away. He'd endured the horrendous pain the disease causes. It was very painful to try and lay still during the MRIs every six weeks. He even fell asleep in the hospital bathroom one time trying to avoid that day's MRI. He'd had to bear the crushing news twice that when he thought he'd beat the disease, it was back. Each of these sufferings elevated Dad's sense of his huge victory of Sunday, February 3, 2013.

An important aspect of losses is that they help us not take the victories for granted. Living life focused only in the moment tends to be human nature. If we can step back and look at the victory as more than just one big moment, the triumph is more special when seen as the culmination of all the loss and work leading up to it. Repeated losses also make it easier to know a huge victory will probably lead again into more work and loss before the next one.

Repeated work and loss of high value before victory is a sad aspect of war. I don't think even the most patriotic American, if there's an alternative, would choose for our country to be at war. If there's another option it's always better to avoid war in favor of peace. To civilians, times of peace and being able to say, "Our country is not at war," are favorable to the times we send our troops to fight even when we know it's to protect our freedoms.

The problem is our country can no longer really say at any time that we are not at war. That's because we are at war with ourselves in many areas throughout our country. It may not be a war sanctioned by Congress, or led by our commander- in- chief, but it's war. Craig and many police officers fight it daily.

Soldiers and police officers share a common bond because both put their lives in a position to serve and protect others at all costs. The sad part is how much we now need police officers to protect us from ourselves. Most of our mid to large -sized cities are such a mess with criminal activity that rather than our officers protecting the masses from a few we ask them daily and nightly to fight a war wherein they are outnumbered and often outgunned. Praise the Lord they are rarely outsmarted! Truly it is by God's grace that the high majority of our officers get to go home to their families and loved ones at the end of each shift. We as civilians who enjoy our "times of peace" should be praying for and supporting our officers as we would any military personnel. We pray for my brother's protection every morning and night as if he were heading into battle.

Craig is clever. As a family we know about his job only what he wants to share with us. He rarely imparts all the nitty-gritty details of exactly what he faces each day. He tells us only what he wants us to know because we really couldn't handle all the information. I think a part of officers' protect-and-serve mentality is to protect all of us from the true gory details of their day-to-day service and the mental anguish those details would cause if our minds had to mull them over and over in an attempt to process the harsh realities. It's a true case of ignorance is bliss. All of us want to be able to walk the streets in our neighborhood feeling safe. We just don't want to know how the streets got to be safe.

I've seen people listening to Craig's stories and watched the reactions they generate. The street war stories are intriguing, cool, and exciting. Everyone listening thinks they know what they would do to come out victorious in the situations. They're sure they'd be so tough and smooth inflicting justice on the many criminals with no conscience they'd have to face down. The truth is few of us could handle it.

Guess who got pretty close to straight A grades in high school and college, Craig or me? Guess who is a great book learner, Craig or me? Guess who was the type of model student public schools were made for, Craig or me? The answers to all three questions are me. Yet I tell my kids all the time I could never be as talented as their uncle; never come close to doing what he does.

If anyone is ever in an emergency and can't remember their US history or parts of speech, I'd be happy to come to their aid. Otherwise I know, despite all my academic knowledge, anyone in distress would want my brother with them over me anytime. The value in what he can and is willing to do far outweighs anything I aced so easily in school.

Because I know this, I never offer my advice to any of his stories he does decide to tell us. I'll ask questions about procedure, what things mean legally, or the background of some criminal to help me even try to understand how some people get to the point they do. The closest I ever come to giving Craig advice is when I've told him, "Hey, you've gotta' do what you need to do so you're the one who goes home that day."

There are plenty of staged cop shows people love to watch on TV, and the general public now makes the mistake of thinking they can do what any real officer does. No cop show, crime novel, or the general public take on police stories we hear can ever come close to actually being in the volatile circumstances every officer has the possibility to face at any moment. Those are moments that, unless they are a part of your own reality, you will never truly know how you would react to and feel about.

Mom, Craig, his wife Jeanette, Jeff, Jen, Chris, me, the grandkids, in-laws, extended family, and friends all had our reactions and feelings about Dad's surgery. But you know who knows what it was like to go into surgery that day? Dad. Only Dad.

Those of us in the pre-op area watched Dad's gurney go down the hall and turn the corner through the double doors into the operating room area. We watched until we couldn't see him being wheeled away anymore. Each of us had a feeling of facing down the unknown, but only Dad actually had to face it. Dad went into surgery full of prayer and peace, hoping and expecting to win, and he did!

After our post-op prayer with the surgeon in the waiting room, we asked for the more specific medical details. Dad was in recovery and would be transported to the Intensive Care Unit (ICU). He had done so well the surgeon debated not putting him on a ventilator but felt it was necessary to make sure Dad's body stayed at a constant resting rate as he went through the process of waking back up after such a major operation.

Mom, Craig, Jeff, Chris, and I moved our base of operations to the ICU waiting room to sit until the nurses could tell us what our next steps would be to help Dad. We were so thrilled Dad was still here and we wanted to savor the victory of surgery, but we all still had the sense of being ready for the battle ahead. We were more than cautiously optimistic but, unfortunately, the huge victory of surviving surgery was not the end of Dad's MRSA story. There was a lot more work to be done.

After a wait of some time, we were so pleased when the nurses told us we could go back quietly a couple at a time to see Dad. We were told to be prepared for a shock, and shocked we each were. The room was dark with only the beeps and whirs of machines. Dad looked beat and drugged. He was unconscious and on a ventilator. We each quietly congratulated him, thanked God over and over in our minds, and then went out to the ICU waiting room to set up vigil. All of us determined without even discussing it that someone would be there at all times until Dad woke up.

Mom—who isn't always in the greatest health herself, who at home thoroughly and deeply sleeps—camped out in the uncomfortable, only semi-clean waiting room for thirty-nine hours. The ICU nurses were very kind and let Mom go see Dad for a few minutes each hour. That was her mission for a day and a half. Dad had done his part in making it through surgery, and she would do her part to wait out the minutes with him until he came back to consciousness.

I spent the first night shift with Mom so she wouldn't be alone. Chris covered the next day, and Craig covered the next night. To allow Mom a little sleep that second night, even if in the cramped waiting room chairs, Craig offered to go visit Dad during the allowed times. He, with his medical training, could handle the ICU environment and Dad's condition objectively. He told me about a one-way conversation he had with Dad that night during which he told Dad how great it would be to wake up the next day because it was Mom's birthday.

I must confess the dates had blurred a little in my mind and February fifth had snuck up and could've passed if Craig hadn't called on his way home from the hospital that morning and said we needed to convince Mom she was leaving the hospital for a little because we were going to have a party for her that night. Craig said Mom wouldn't want to, but he also said we needed to, so I should call Jeff, get our whole families together, and tell Mom the time to be home.

I got plans in motion for that and then, having been made aware of what date it actually was, got the kids in motion for a birthday breakfast. A bit later we surprised Mom in the waiting room with some nonhospital food for breakfast, a birthday balloon, and a dozen purple roses with a card we had signed from Dad since he couldn't get them himself that day. We visited for a while, got the latest status on Dad, and Mom agreed to come home for just two hours that night, if at all possible, since we were insistent.

My kids are hospital troopers. They can stick out long visits when they need to but greatly prefer short ones. Given the crowded conditions of the waiting room, we didn't stay long after our birthday breakfast but headed back to Mom and Dad's. The phone rang at Mom and Dad's not much later, around 1:30 p.m. Mom was very excited to tell me she couldn't talk but was so thrilled the nurses had just told her they were pulling Dad's vent. She had wanted to call quickly so I would know, pray, and tell Craig and Jeff. After the ten-second call, she rushed into Dad's ICU room to be there for him. The vent was pulled and Dad slowly woke up. What a birthday present from Dad to Mom!

It turns out Dad, as he had put it, did have a deal with God. He and God had talked about Dad not waking up on a ventilator and Dad never did. When I had been told postsurgery Dad was on the vent, I had been a little bit disappointed because I had seen how hopeful Dad was that he wouldn't be. Of course, I had forgotten God always has the best plans and timing. Dad had needed his body to be on a ventilator for a time, and God knew ahead of time Dad would need to be, but he had not woken up on it. Dad still doesn't remember being on the ventilator. The deal was Dad wouldn't wake up on a vent and he didn't. What a blessing when our God, who doesn't have to, gives us special treats like that.

Why did I feel that bit of disappointment about Dad's ventilator minutes after the huge victory of surgery? Because we all have to be reminded in life to not be like the Israelites. God can do wondrous big things, and moments later we are doubting Him for the small things.

The Israelites had been slaves in Egypt for over three hundred years. They cried out to God and He heard and promised to deliver them from their situation. God described the work He was going to do for the Israelite people to Moses, who He was sending to help carry out His mission, in this way, "Therefore, say to the Israelites: I am the Lord, and I will bring you out from under the yoke of the Egyptians. I will free you from being slaves to them, and I will redeem you with an outstretched arm and with mighty acts of judgment. I will take you as my own people, and I will be your God. Then you will know that I am the Lord your God, who brought you out from under the yoke of the Egyptians. And I will bring you to the land I swore with uplifted hand to give to Abraham, to Isaac and to Jacob. I will give it to you as a possession. I am the Lord." (Exodus chapter 6, verses 6–8)

God fulfilled all those promises to the Israelites, and they left Egypt as one large group heading to live in the new land God had planned for them. The Israelites had witnessed devastating plagues God sent to cripple Egypt. They had seen the Pharaoh of the powerful nation agree to let them leave. Then, as they were fleeing, they looked back to see the Egyptian army pursuing them. Completely discounting all God had just miraculously done to secure their departure, the Israelites turned to Moses and complained. That quickly they forgot all God had recently done and doubted Him.

God saved the Israelites by drowning the Egyptian army in the sea and He continued to care for the Israelites for the next forty years until they were allowed to take possession of the land He had promised their ancestors hundreds of years before. During that forty years, while God showed faithfulness after faithfulness, the Israelites continued to grumble and worry after each providence from God.

I had always been critical of the Israelites when I studied their story in the Bible. How could they be such whiners and complainers? The sad thing is that as each of the events of Dad's postsurgery days in the hospital crept up on us with unexpected quickness, our first responses tended to be momentary panic before we reminded ourselves that God, again, would help us through the situation.

Originally Dad was supposed to be in the ICU for a week to ten days. When he came off the vent, Mom was told he would be moving to a regular floor within hours. It was almost time for Mom to arrive home for her birthday party and she called us in a hurried panic. They were releasing Dad to a regular floor less than two days out of his surgery and she was running around the hospital trying to make sure Dad could get a private room. That was all we heard until she actually made it to her party two hours later.

Of course, God had gone before her. When Mom arrived up on the seventh floor of the hospital ready to make calls and beg for a private room, she met the kind nurses who had cared for Dad before his surgery. They were all so thankful to hear he had come through surgery successfully and they told her they would get him a private room that evening no matter what and it would be their privilege to take care of him. Mom told us the story around their dining room table during her birthday dinner and wanted to cry with happiness, wondering out loud to us once again, "Why do we ever doubt?"

The next day Mom called to see if I could come up for a bit so she could run home, actually take a long awaited shower, and get some things Dad needed now that he was in a regular room. I was a little worried to be the one responsible at the hospital but I said I'd be right there. Mom assured me Dad would be resting, there was nothing that should go on, and she would be back soon. I was happy to get to say "Hi" to Dad for the first time since his surgery.

Our postsurgery greeting, the one where this book idea was born, was very brief because his nurse entered and announced they were taking away his pain pump and he'd get a couple painkillers every few hours. Dad was less than three days out of surgery with a completely rebuilt back. He looked at me and told me that couldn't happen. I panicked on the inside but on the outside headed to the halls to find the nurse, get a hold of Dad's doctor, and find out some information.

Before we could get the information we needed about the pain pump question, an x-ray team showed up in Dad's room and announced they were taking him downstairs for an x-ray. When asked if he thought he could get on the stretcher himself, I could tell Dad wanted to say, "Are you kidding me?" He instead politely said, "No, I don't think so," and they scooped him up abruptly, flopped him on his back on the stretcher, and banged him into a few doors and walls on the way downstairs.

The x-ray department was backed up and I waited with Dad suffering in great pain on the stretcher in the hallway for almost an hour. I only walked away for a few moments each time trying to find a place in the basement with cell phone reception so I could get Mom back to the hospital as soon as possible. Dad eventually made it through the x-ray with minimal grimacing and was then banged along the halls again on the way back to his room.

I was hoping the panic moments would quit coming, but right after we got back to the room, some surgical residents showed up to examine Dad's back. They rolled him to the side and told him they were going to take the dressing off. I knew Dad had been told that should stay on for a week, and Dad knew that, too. We both questioned them enough that they agreed to leave it for the time being and not rip it off that day.

Mom returned shortly after the residents' departure and took over as the point person again for Dad. Even walking out of the hospital, I knew God had each detail of that three hours I'd just been through worked out beforehand and I told myself I needed to be more grateful and keep remembering God's faithfulness during the small crises and not only afterwards.

There were fewer surprises the next few days of Dad's hospital stay and things even seemed to fall into a bit of a routine. Mom spent the week getting home around midnight and sleeping until 5:00 a.m. I would wake her up to get back to the hospital so she could be with Dad when the morning doctors came in to check Dad and give her and him any new information.

Dad was not going to be able to be released from the hospital and go directly home. He would need some time at a rehab center to learn to move again. Given Dad's delicate medical condition, Mom was really researching and putting a lot of prayer into where Dad should be transported. The healthcare aspect was just as important as the rehab aspect of whatever institution would be taking care of Dad's recovery.

The Saturday following Dad's surgery, Mom decided it would be all right to sleep a few extra hours because doctors don't make routine rounds, and generally no new healthcare decisions are made on the weekend. At ten o'clock the phone rang with a nurse telling Mom that Dad would be discharged within the hour and asking if she had a preference as to where he should be transported.

There we went into panic mode again! It's never a crazy paralyzing panic mode any of us go into, it's just a determined we-need-to-address-this-thoroughly-and-now mode that we go into. Nonetheless, the adrenaline and blood pressure definitely went up each time we felt spurred into action we weren't ready for. Mom and I left immediately for the hospital to be there within the hour we were told we had. Three hours later we were all still in Dad's hospital room waiting for his transport.

Mom and Dad had made a decision about which rehab facility they thought would be best for Dad and he was eventually transported there that day. I followed the ambulance from the hospital and Jeff met us at the facility. Dad had been given no pain medication Saturday morning in anticipation of his transport and upon arrival he couldn't be given any until he was properly checked in. Being the weekend, the facility workers were few and far between and moving slowly, so we sat with Dad for another two hours before anyone came to see him.

Dad was really in pain by the time an aid arrived and we tried to tell her that he was six days out of major surgery, still had MRSA pain, and really needed some relief. She was more interested in finding out what belongings Dad was bringing to the facility and if he had any bruises or marks on his skin before arrival. We answered all of her inane questions on behalf of Dad and then asked again if she would be able to get him some relief from his pain soon. She informed us they were not a medical facility and she wasn't concerned with Dad's health or pain issues. Their job would be to help him be walking again within the next two to three weeks and she would go see if there was a nurse available who might be able to help us with our health questions.

At her departure I looked at Dad and said, "Two to three weeks, huh?"

He answered back, "I'll make it out of here in two."

The group of us was bordering on hostility as another hour dragged on with Dad lying there. Close to 9:00 that night, Mom finally had to call their family doctor, who was not a part of the facility staff, to tell him what was transpiring and ask if he could run interference. Thankfully their doctor did and by about midnight we felt safe to leave Dad until early the next morning. Waiting out those hours, I had to remind myself and then say aloud to the rest of them, "We can't be like the Israelites."

The God of the Exodus had delivered Dad through an amazing surgery and we needed to continually and purposefully trust Him with all the minor details that kept being hurled our way.

CHAPTER SEVEN

Football - A game well played
War - People on the home front
God's Word - Blessings in the hardship

There is satisfaction in a game well played. If a player has performed well during an entire game, the victory has a better feel than a win barely squeaked out after a whole game of sloppy play. Any win is fun for the moment, but when you look back later and analyze the game, the analysis that shows consistent and good technique is much more satisfying.

Football teams and coaches train during the off-season and every weekday during the season in the hopes of playing the perfect game. While there may never be a perfect game, even being a part of one where each aspect of play came together at just the right moments is rewarding. It's fun to see a game like that played out live. It's also fun to watch videotape of it later and see each little part that resulted in victory.

Coaches from peewee up to pro will sit down very soon after a game and intently delve into the video of their team's most recent performance. They're looking for each play, good or bad, that led to the game's outcome. Our family can sit around for hours after our pickup games analyzing our own good and bad plays.

The year Chris and I were engaged, we combined families for the year's Thanksgiving football game. Chris is tech-savvy so he set up a fancy for-the-early-nineties system — a VHS camcorder on a tripod — to record the game. The ground at his mom and dad's house was very wet so the camcorder sat on the front sidewalk to film us playing football a half an acre down the yard.

All of us were still muddy and cold from the game when we put the tape into his parent's VCR to watch on their big screen projection TV. The faraway field recording system had caught blurry images of us running, passing, and tackling, except for the time the heavy wind blew the camera over and we only recorded grass for a bit. The entire tape was watched to the sound of wind rushing past the camcorder microphone, interrupted by a few extra loud shouts and celebrations that it picked up from the field.

Regardless, we sat muddy in Chris's parents' living room for at least an hour, stopping and starting that tape and having a great time analyzing every move we very amateur players made. Then we did the same thing on the much smaller TV in the family room of Mom and Dad's basement for the next few days. There were some hits on each other so hard that we could see the blurry recipients recoil and we watched and exclaimed about those over and over.

Even with today's filming techniques, the view from the sidelines during a game is combined with noise, movement everywhere, obstructions of sightline, and play calls to be made. Later, when coaches are watching tape they can rewind, pause, and fast forward to catch all the details they missed at real life speed. They not only see again the huge third down pass the quarterback threw for a completion, they also see each offensive lineman fighting off a rushing opponent which was what gave the quarterback time to make the pass. They not only see again the running back sprint for a twenty-yard gain, they also see how two linemen pushed aside hulking defensive players to create a space just large enough for that running back to squeeze through. They not only see again the completed field goal that kept them in close point range, they also see the hands of the defensemen across the line that narrowly missed blocking the ball.

In the midst of a live situation it's hard to focus on the little happenings leading up to the big finale, but when we have the time later to sit back and remember all the little moments involved, then the finale is even more meaningful. It's difficult in the middle of a significant life event to see all the people involved. The players that draw attention, like the quarterbacks in a game, get all the notice, not the blockers and guards holding their line or even the center who gets the quarterback the ball time after time to make the noticeable flashy plays.

When America entered World War II after the attack on Pearl Harbor, the surge of men wanting to enlist was massive. Americans were ready to defend our country and newsreels showed recruiting areas filled with eager soldiers-to-be leaving for deployment overseas. In the middle of the rush to defend our country, people's main focus was on the individuals going off to Europe and the South Pacific. Years later, when World War II could be looked back upon and analyzed, the efforts of all that Americans did at home really stood out as one of our proudest patriotic times. Those on the home front worked very hard so the soldiers overseas could be supported.

Mom's mom and dad, Lillian and Arthur Markoff (we called them Gram and Pop), were married on September 6, 1941. On December 7th, Pearl Harbor was bombed. Pop and his brother Marco, both first-generation Americans, volunteered their services. Marco enlisted in the Army in early 1942 and Pop was accepted into flight school for the Air Force. Pop was sent to an Air Force base in Lubbock, Texas. Gram went with him, lived in an area boarding house, and got a job. Pop never completed his training because, while in Texas, they were contacted by Pop's family back in Wilmerding, Pennsylvania.

Pop's mom had become ill a few years before. Pop's dad had now taken ill and would be unable to care for Pop's siblings anymore. Marco was already deployed to the Italian front and Pop's four younger siblings needed care at home. Pop wanted to be among the groups of men heading out to fight and he had an important choice to make. Pop's choice was for his siblings. Pop was honorably discharged and he and Gram returned to Pennsylvania. In the midst of a big war, which was the whole nation's focus, there was a little family back home that needed help and Gram and Pop chose to see that.

They moved back to Pennsylvania from Texas in 1943 and, instead of airplanes, Pop drove his dad's bread routes. Gram, a little over two years into marriage, became a mom to Pop's younger brother and three younger sisters and spent her days wholeheartedly raising them. She told me on wash days she would do up to fourteen loads of laundry and definitely an entire load of white bobby socks that had to be all matched up when they were clean.

World War II was the focus of our country in the early 1940s, and Pop and Gram supported America and prayed for Marco overseas. Their job of helping their family in need at the same time our country was in need was never going to be noticed right then. After the big event of World War II was no longer the main focus in life, family members could look back and see the sacrifice Gram and Pop made, not in battle, but in seeing family as an important part of what made America strong in the first place. The ideals Americans in Europe were fighting for needed to be preserved in wartime so that they were intact for the soldiers to come home to. Fighting for a country that fell apart while you fought for it wouldn't have been much of a sweet victory.

Pilots, infantry, and medics returning postwar all had wounds seen and unseen to recover from and stories to share. These stories passed down through generations as family legacies. Included in the stories our family told over the years about World War II was the one of Gram and Pop coming home to care for Pop's siblings. Their sacrifice during the war years was an example to us as my brothers and I grew up and Pop always told us, "Family is the most important thing." Their sacrifice continued to be appreciated even when Gram was in her eighties and her sisters-in-law in their sixties and seventies would call her on the phone and say, "Hi, Mum," when she answered because that's what she had been to them.

Gram and Pop put in a lot of hard work over the years raising Pop's siblings and yet, in the midst of it, there were blessings. The biggest visible blessing to be seen was a family incredibly close-knit through the years. Another blessing was that their actions taught the rest of us that when family needs you, you come.

Gram and Pop went home in 1943. Growing up, and even after I was grown, Mom and Dad made many jump in the car at a moment's notice trips to Pennsylvania when Gram and Pop had a need. Now it's been my turn to willingly be ready to head across the states and get to Michigan whenever Mom and Dad say it's needed.

These small blessings amidst hardships are often only noticed later when God gives us a calmer time in life to reflect back on what we've come through. Solomon was a king blessed by God with great wisdom. Solomon had every material possession possible. There was political peace for the first time in Israel's history, and much time to study and learn.

Despite this, he was troubled by the world around him and bogged down by all the hardships he saw in life that caused him to cry out that all aspects of life were meaningless. He wrote in Ecclesiastes chapter 9, verse 12, "Moreover, no man knows when his hour will come: As fish are caught in a cruel net, or birds are taken in a snare, so men are trapped by evil times that fall unexpectedly upon them."

We know hardships are going to come repeatedly in life. It's the result of living in a sinful world. Solomon wrestled with this until he, in his God-given wisdom, was able to conclude in Ecclesiastes, chapter 12, verses 13 and 14, "Now all has been heard; here is the conclusion of the matter: Fear God and keep his commandments, for this is the whole duty of man. For God will bring every deed into judgment, including every hidden thing, whether it is good or evil."

When life has hardships, we must take time to follow God and be able to see the blessings He places within the hardships. When we look back at the time surrounding Dad's surgery, we see blessings we couldn't have seen at the time when our main focus was Dad's survival.

One blessing was the prayers and thoughts of extended family and friends—even friends of friends we had never met. I had no time to talk to anyone except immediate family for weeks, but once he was back in Pennsylvania Chris could and he would tell us about the many prayers people were saying for us.

Dad has the blessing of a great group of male friends who all rallied around him and checked in with him often. Some came to pray with him the night before surgery. After the surgery, while Dad was getting better, none got offended if he didn't have time or energy to call them. They would just take the initiative and show up. They called Mom to make sure she was all right. They came and handicap-equipped the house for Dad when he returned from rehab. Many, many meals and trays of cookies were left on Mom and Dad's doorstep for us during our stay.

The numerous lessons learned by my kids turned out to be a very big blessing. They learned to rise to expectations and take care of each other. My kids ranged in age from fourteen months to fourteen years at the time of Dad's surgery, and I think they had been left on their own once. During our six weeks in Michigan, they were constantly and unexpectedly being asked to hold down things at Mom and Dad's on their own while Mom and I took care of rotations at the hospital and rehab center or ran errands to make sure we had all the supplies and equipment needed for when Dad came home.

Another blessing is that the kids learned quickly that life will not always be—and doesn't have to be—just about them. Once they saw that and could put each other first, they were able to also see that others wanted to be a blessing to them, too. They had the blessing of being cared for by their Aunt Beth and Uncle Mark and older cousins, Molly and Matt, the day of Dad's surgery. They had the blessing of Molly who would stop by Mom and Dad's to check in and stay with them sometimes when I had to leave. An added blessing to spending extra time with her was that she could also drive to their favorite fast food restaurants for them!

The kids knew they were being a blessing to Mom who never had to come home to an empty house late at night the entire time Dad was away, which eased his mind while he recovered. They also realized the blessing of extra playtime with cousins that we always want to see more of every time we're in Michigan.

Because Emily was the oldest, and a teenager I suppose, many people asked her, "Don't you want to get back to your life?" I could tell how much Emily had learned when she told Mom and me she knew what the people meant but didn't they realize that her life couldn't exist without her? She wanted to tell people that what she was in Michigan doing for Mom and Dad was her life and that was exactly where she was supposed to be at the time, but she knew it would sound sassy coming from her so she didn't.

Sometimes a hardship will hit within a hardship, but there are blessings to be seen even there. Dad had been settled into rehab for a couple of days. I was actually having a calmer day at

Mom and Dad's, and Craig and his family were visiting. Craig's daughter, Maria—along with Emily and our second oldest daughter, Abigail—were screaming and running around us adults in the living room playing hide-and-seek when Jen called my cell phone. Her voice was absolute panic. She had dropped her children off at her sister's house and was heading an hour away to work. Her sister called to tell her that Lauren was in a seizure and paramedics were on the way. Jen was crying that she wouldn't be able to get to Lauren fast enough and didn't know what was going to happen to her.

I covered the mouthpiece as she talked and told Craig across the room what was going on because I knew if anyone could get to Lauren, he could. Within seconds he found out where Lauren was being transported, met the ambulance as she was being wheeled into the emergency room, flashed his police badge, and never left her until Jeff and Jen could arrive.

That phone call, with all we had been through recently with Dad, felt like a gut punch to every one of us. When I ran outside to move our van so Craig could get his car out, I remember yelling out loud, "Please, Lord, don't let anything happen to Lauren!" We'd all just been through a crisis with Dad and none of us wanted our very special four-year-old to be in crisis now.

Had Dad not been in rehab and had we not been in town, Craig probably wouldn't have been down visiting on a weekday. Even in the shock of this new hardship, God gave us the blessing of having Craig be nearby so that our niece had the blessing of never being alone. Jeff and Jen had the blessing of knowing Lauren would be watched over until they got to her.

One of my favorite Bible stories is in the book of Second Kings in chapter 6. Elisha, a prophet of God, and his servant woke up one morning to see the city they were in surrounded by an enemy army that was looking specifically for Elisha. The servant panicked but Elisha prayed. In his prayer, Elisha asked God to open the eyes of his servant and God did. When the servant looked up he was able to see the hills surrounding the enemy army full of the horses and chariots of fire of the army of the Lord. Elisha had told his servant, "Don't be afraid. Those who are with us are more than those who are with them."

When we truly open our eyes and focus on God, we can see His care surrounding us. Big moments can require singular focus and during intense events, it's not a natural instinct to inspect every aspect and gain lessons from them. The natural instinct is to simply survive. We've learned as a family, however, that we've got to look for the blessings from the hand of God at the same time we go through the big moments. It's amazing how we find them every time.

CHAPTER EIGHT

Football - Monday morning quarterback
War - Returning home
God's Word - After the mountaintop

"Monday morning quarterback" is a football term but it has carried over into many aspects of life. A Monday morning quarterback looks back at a situation and tells how it should've been handled. Different from the Sunday quarterback who has to react in real-time in the game and make quick decisions without the knowledge of how all the other people and variables in a situation will play out, the Monday morning quarterback has the advantage of hindsight to assess a situation.

People like to play Monday morning quarterback because it makes them feel superior. Entire sports and news channels are devoted to Monday morning quarterback programming. Games are analyzed and critiqued over and over and over again by newscasters who weren't a part of them.

Fans are also exceptional Monday morning quarterbacks, my family included. Our family has a favorite team going on four generations now and it is predetermined for our kids even before birth where their loyalty will lie. Our two-year-old, Caleb, can already pick out the team logo anywhere he sees it. Due to our familial devotion to our favorite franchise, we excel at Monday morning quarterbacking them. A frequent comment by our family in the weekly analysis of our favorite team's performance is that they always play to the level of their competition. If they play a team projected to beat them, they seem to rise to the occasion. Then the next week, when their matchup is against a team that hasn't won any games, our favorite team will play unbelievably badly and lose.

We also don't like it when our favorite team tries too often to run the same old running back up the middle play. It's extremely rare that the play ever amounts to a gain in yardage. We watch them line up, hand the ball off, and almost every time see the running back hit a brick wall of defensemen.

Of course, we can give our opinions after the fact, but we weren't in the game and didn't see what the players saw as the team lined up each down. We have the privilege of time to look back and see what they didn't see.

A huge annoyance when I am playing a game of football with family or friends is to have a pass intercepted. I wish I could get the ball back and have the pass never thrown. Announcers of television games are always commenting after interceptions that the ball should've never been thrown. Great insight. If the quarterback knew the ball was going to be intercepted, he wouldn't have thrown it. It's disappointing when a play, or really anything we attempt in life, doesn't go the way we hope and comments by people afterward can never change the already completed situation.

The Monday morning quarterback craze by people shows how automatic it has become for all of us to pass judgment on others. I think it used to be most people truly wanted to make their comments well-meaning, with thoughts of the other person first. Because of such an increase in selfishness in our culture, a person playing Monday morning quarterback, in any situation of life, thinks of elevating himself first and the person being critiqued as of lesser importance. Advice is truly only well-meaning if it benefits the recipient first. If it benefits the ego of the giver first, then it's not really advice.

Soldiers go off to deployment or war with hopes that they will defend their country honorably and successfully. Events are what they are during their time of service and then they must return home. Many soldiers have their own personal issues to wrestle with when they get home, and often have to do it while listening to comments from people who weren't there and have no idea how events transpired. It's especially hard because these comments are from people that the soldiers left and went to war to protect.

Whether we agree with a cause or war our soldiers are sent to confront, those of us who were not there should still tell any soldier we meet, "Thank you." My father-in-law, John, is good at doing this. Anytime he sees someone in a military uniform at a restaurant or store, he will initiate conversation by thanking them for their service. We don't know what any soldier has been through in their time away from America, and many don't want to talk to civilians or even their family about it. One reason may be that our advice to them about situations we really know nothing about would be no help to them at all. However, we can still say a simple, "Thank you."

A couple years ago my family helped host a Christmas luncheon for some veterans because we wanted to do something special to thank them for being willing to fight for our country. They came from a variety of service areas and we had a wonderful afternoon serving and talking with them. A part of the afternoon we didn't expect was the gratefulness of the Vietnam veterans for having been invited. They had gone off to Vietnam as a duty to America and as a service to its citizens. They returned home after a hard war to American citizens who were not grateful for the soldiers' service and whose comments in the hindsight of the war were not at all helpful to soldiers who just wanted to get back home to the country whose ideals they had defended.

The Vietnam veterans we served were especially grateful for the afternoon luncheon because, they said, to hear a simple "Thank you" that day was the exact opposite of what they returned home to in America forty years earlier. We were humbled as a family to have been able to give them a small thank-you that had been a long time in coming.

Being thrown into our six weeks in Michigan, the kids and I had a small glimpse of the coming home disconnect that many soldiers probably feel. We felt like we had just been through a very personal battle as a family and the instant I walked into our house after the drive home, I felt drained. The adrenaline and heightened sense of urgency I had been living on for six weeks was instantly gone and I was exhausted.

People were excited to see us back and everyone's first questions were, "How are you?" "How is your dad?" or both questions asked without a break between for me to answer. All the busyness and range of emotions we had been through could not really be conveyed with the usual one-word answer given to those questions. I knew all our casual acquaintances didn't really want the full explanation that would completely answer their questions. They were really saying, "It's good to see you back." They were not prepared for, or interested in, the deeper and more personal thoughts and emotions we could have shared with them.

I couldn't even describe to good friends all that had transpired while we were away. On top of that I felt bad, but I didn't really care what had happened with our friends and in the area while we were gone. Emily, Joseph, and Abigail all felt similar and mentioned how everyone else had just lived their lives for the last six weeks and that was how we would've been had we never gone to Michigan. We looked back at all we had accomplished and learned and it was hard to settle back into school each day, church on Sundays, and the daily schedule of extra activities. We still enjoyed all of them but for a while they just didn't seem important.

I definitely went through a period of *I just didn't care* when I returned home. If something was not of true consequence in life, I had a hard time having any motivation to do it. In addition, I had a hard time gearing up any emotion to care about complaints or worries others shared with me if I saw them as trivial and, for a long time, if something was not of life-or-death importance, I considered it all trivial.

Another struggle in our relationships upon our return home was committing to events or responsibilities that were any point in the future. I remember feeling real panic when I had to decide about invitations or events more than a few days away because I still had that sense that if Mom or Dad called at any minute we'd be gone again. The kids and I had returned home and we didn't look or act outwardly different, but inwardly we were permanently different.

There is camaraderie in crisis, and sometimes we want to push away anyone who didn't sit in the trenches with us. It is hard to allow yourself to rest, relax, and slowly let others you knew before the crisis back into your lives. It is important to learn to do this, though, or you will get stuck acting as if you were still in the moments of crisis, and that will become an exhausting way to live.

Dad has found a great way, I think, to accomplish not alienating others, and that is to steer the conversation away from himself. Even if you have been, or are, in a tough time, you don't always have to redirect a conversation to be about you. I have seen people ask Dad time and time again with great concern how he's doing and within a few sentences of conversation Dad has asked them a question about themselves and completely turned the conversation from his current health issues. Dad just does this naturally because he's a caring person, but I can see there is a benefit about it: it helps Dad not fixate on his circumstances while keeping a connection with people who care about him but could never fully imagine his situation even if he described it to them for hours.

The hard reality that life immediately moves on after impacting events is the fact that Dad's surgery was now three years ago. That time in our life is still at the front of our minds if not daily, at least weekly, and yet three years have passed so quickly. I always feel so good when I sit down and get a chance to write some of Mom and Dad's story, but those times have been few and far between.

I sat down today determined to write because Mom and Dad are arriving at our house in two weeks. I was two sentences into what I hoped would be a good long writing time and into the room where I was unusually by myself walked my now four-year-old, Hannah, to show off her costume-jeweled ring on each finger and discuss where she got each one. Maybe I'm wrong and I should kick her out and tell her Mommy is busy but I don't. Five minutes later my ten-year-old, Sarah, walked in with her church club book to discuss answers she was looking up in the Bible.

"Are you busy, Mom? I can come back."

"No, not at all," I answer.

That answer leads to another ten-minute pause of this book to read her Bible with her and listen to the verses she has memorized. Then in fifteen minutes it's time to leave and help with the church club.

Add up lots of moments like the ones with Hannah and Sarah and soon three years have passed. Should I have a book written or conversations and moments the kids and I can recall together? Dad and Mom would say the moments, and so it has been— though I am excited to finally be giving them their story.

The same reason there's been no book is the same reason I don't always get a workout, have a bigger garden, sleep much, or read books for myself. But going back to chapter three of our story, great kids, like anything great, won't just happen. We have six terrific ones and the work of them has come before a book.

It is easy to feel guilty about that in today's world, but God was in each of those feeling guilty moments with me. After a life-changing experience, it's hard to feel OK just doing everyday life and imagine that could be all God wants you to be doing. Everyday life is not unimportant. It's what builds the foundation for the extraordinary events.

The world will always make us question our priorities and where to place our time. That's another reason to remember God is in charge of the moments and we need to do our best to look for His presence and live each one for Him no matter the circumstance and no matter when we feel like we have a responsibility to finish something else.

God has a time for everything, and we have to relax in that knowledge. I believe there is a time when this book will be done. I believe there is a time when I will exercise all I want to, have a bigger garden, sleep all night, or read a book for pleasure. I also know there will be a time too soon when our six terrific kids will be all grown up. The above list can wait until God's time because those things can all be done at any time.

Postsurgery Mom and Dad's lives, too, took on what Mom soon began calling, "a new normal." They had to learn to not feel guilty when, because of Dad's health on a particular day, they just couldn't make an event. They had to adjust to the fact that getting anywhere was going to take a lot more effort because it takes a lot more effort just for Dad to get his body moving each morning. Mom and Dad had returned home after the surgery and they were the same people, but few aspects of their life would ever be the same.

In these new realities of settling back into a regular sort of scheduled life, we saw firsthand the importance of what God instituted for His people back in the book of Exodus as a Sabbath rest. The beginning of the book of Genesis tells the account of God creating the world in six days and then resting on the seventh. His rest was to be our example of a Sabbath rest. Years later, after the Exodus, when He spoke the Ten Commandments to the Israelites recorded in Exodus, chapter 20, He told them that the Sabbath was to be a lasting ordinance between Him and His people. The idea of a purposeful rest after periods of work is exactly what God knows we need.

Our family had been through what is often called a mountaintop experience. We were living in a busy, event-filled time that kept our senses and bodies in a constant state of alertness like hikers climbing to the top of a high peak. We had stayed perched at the top of the mountain in a state of busyness and readiness for weeks waiting until the time to come down.

Our human bodies cannot physically sustain the experience of being continuously on the mountaintop. There will come a time when we have to climb down from the mountaintop and ease back into life in the valley below. Our lives off the mountaintop may look different from before our climb, but with rest and prayer we are able to settle back into a new normal.

CHAPTER NINE

Football, war, and God's Word - Something bigger than yourself

Football teams are made up of individual players who work together to achieve a win. Wars are fought by individual soldiers who, together, defend their country to the best of their abilities. God's Word is a chronology of ordinary people used by God to accomplish amazing outcomes. Each of these, football, war, and God's Word, in increasing importance of their impact on eternity, can teach us that every one of us can be a part of something bigger than ourselves.

Selfishness and self-focus make for a narrow-minded way to live. The popular concept of looking out for number one may be very intriguing, but it leads to an empty life and results in very little impact on eternity. Jesus's first sermon recorded in the Bible begins with a section called the Beatitudes. The book of Matthew records these words of Jesus in chapter 5, verses 3 through 10:

> *Blessed are the poor in spirit,*
> *for theirs is the kingdom of heaven.*
> *Blessed are those who mourn,*

for they will be comforted.
Blessed are the meek,
for they will inherit the earth.
Blessed are those who hunger and thirst for righteousness,
for they will be filled.
Blessed are the merciful,
for they will be shown mercy.
Blessed are the pure in heart,
for they shall see God.
Blessed are the peacemakers,
for they will be called sons of God.
Blessed are those who are persecuted because of righteousness,
for theirs is the kingdom of heaven.

None of these attitudes for a blessed life focus on the concept of wallowing in self. Of course we care for and love ourselves, but that should be so we can be used effectively by God in service to others. God has a special plan for each of our lives that is something bigger than we could ever achieve just trying to rely on our own doing. We can't see the miracles God wants to do in our lives if we are focused only on ourselves.

Mom and Dad are a constant example of being able to see beyond themselves to be able to be used by God. Dad can hardly walk and rarely does without a walker, and yet he will still stop at a door and open it for someone else to get through. Dad's shoulders have pretty much been eaten apart by MRSA, and yet if he sees someone struggling to lift or carry something, he offers to help in any way he can. That often means resting objects on his walker and pushing them for people, but it is still a big help to others. Many times his hands don't work much better than his shoulders, and yet he and Mom are always cooking meals for an elderly individual going through health problems or families who have a sick family member or a new baby.

Mom and Dad all but top the list when it comes to medical issues, but they are always praying for and mentioning with true concern people they know who are struggling in ways that can hardly compare to what Mom and Dad have gone through. Mom and Dad would never see it that way: they just see someone else with a need and want to help in any way they can.

Many people from doctors to strangers on the street who see Dad refusing to give up trying to do things in life will praise him, and Dad has realized it is sometimes a great way to open up lines of communication about Christianity that otherwise would not be opened if Dad were just breezing through life with the appearance of any healthy person. He and Mom have come to realize that the many hours of sitting in exam rooms, waiting rooms, hospital rooms, and being pretty slow to walk anywhere they go are part of God's plan to provide opportunities for conversations that wouldn't take place if they were speeding along each day not having any reason to connect with others. Right now Mom and Dad continue to weekly be a witness for God with every medical treatment and appointment they attend. (The types of appointments they had thought might be at an end after Dad's successful surgery.)

It's been hard to decide how to end Dad and Mom's story because although we rejoice in the miracle that Dad survived the surgery, it doesn't mean everything has been perfect. Dad required two more small back surgeries to repair stress fractures above the welded sites and needed to have kyphoplasty. He is now always on oxygen and has been in and out of the hospital numerous times when his breathing, as he says, "goes south." The stays last at least a week, sometimes three, to get his breathing heading back north again—especially when, as often happens, his lungs fill with pneumonia.

The prednisone continues to take a toll on his body and, since he is no longer a candidate for any invasive surgery, he lives with a deteriorated knee and hip that hardly support him and cause major pain whenever he moves. Last week his good shoulder spontaneously fractured.

Mom and Dad's most recent "new normal" is they've moved their bedroom to the main floor of the house and installed an electric chair lift along the railing on the back steps to the door so Dad can leave the house sometimes. Their new realization is that on any day it now takes Dad a couple hours to get ready and out of the house. They can also count on the fact that he will be absolutely exhausted when he returns.

Though many of us think of Dad as a great example of the attitude we want to have when faced with any adversity in life, he is not superhuman. Granted a big portion of his physical body is rebuilt, but he is still not superhuman. Even Dad says it's all right to have a "Why me, God?" moment and cry. It's not a sin to not always be stoic.

It is hard for Dad to get going every day, but he does it. He does it even when a lot of people would not blame him for giving up and spending days at a time in bed. He does it because he knows whatever circumstance he is at in life, he is there because God wants to use that circumstance as a testimony. If Dad gives up and focuses on his own daily pain and medical issues, then those things can no longer help him be a witness for God. We all pray Dad would be completely healed but that doesn't seem to be the bigger plan that God has for him right now.

Because Dad does put effort into every day, and Mom right alongside him, they are a great example of being a part of something bigger than themselves. They give each day to God to be used for Him in every moment. Mom and Dad have learned to see the miracles God does in their every day lives and, because of that, they live their lives feeling very blessed. As Dad says, "There are good days and not-so-good days, but there's never a bad day as long as you have your hand in God's."

REFERENCES

1. L.H. Everts and Company and Ohio Genealogical Society, Tuscarawas Chapter, *Historical Atlas, Tuscarawas County, Ohio, 1875 and 1908 (Combined)*. Strasburg, OH: Gordon Print, 1973.